LAKEHURST:
BARRENS, BLIMPS
& BARONS

LAKEHURST:
BARRENS, BLIMPS & BARONS

THE TRUE TALE OF A PINE BARRENS TOWN

By Eric San Juan

Published in the United States of America

By Eric San Juan

ericsanjuan@gmail.com

www.ericsanjuan.com

Cover photo by Murray Becker.

Cover design by Eric San Juan and Stephen Segal.

Interior photos are either public domain, by Eric San Juan, or property of their respective copyright holders. Many photos provided courtesy of Lakehurst Historical Society (lakehurstnj.org), via *The Manchester Times*. Most military photos from the U.S. Naval Historical Center. Hindenburg photos include work by Murray Becker, Sam Shere, Bill Deekes, Charles Hoff, Guy Pasquarella, Jack Snyder, or Bill Springfield. If you believe a photo has been incorrectly credited or used in error, please contact the author at ericsanjuan@gmail.com.

TABLE OF CONTENTS

PREFACE

I am not an historian. Historians sift through tattered old newspapers and research two hundred-year-old property deeds. They know how to dig up the hidden remnants of our past. They know how to conduct research. They can find needles in haystacks. In short, historians *work*.

Me, I'm just someone who likes to tell stories. In this case *true* stories, but stories nonetheless. Save "historian" for the people who've earned the title. Instead, sit back, turn the pages and let me tell you some of what I've heard about the town of Lakehurst.

Why Lakehurst? Because it makes for a fascinating topic. Sure, you know about the Hindenburg disaster – who doesn't? – but there is much more to this town than one famous event. Though only one square mile, the town has a rich history that extends far beyond its own borders. Doings in Lakehurst played a major role in the development of central New Jersey, military operations during World War II, and more. Lakehurst helped bring people and industry to the most desolate and remote portion of New Jersey and in doing so changed the face of the state.

But most of all I chose Lakehurst because it's personal. I spent more than a decade of my youth here, romping through the woods and picking blueberries and exploring the nooks and crannies of this little community with Matt and Chris and Art and Mike and other names that are meaningless to you but which mean a great deal to me.

Lakehurst is special. To me, and hopefully to you, too.

Even after I grew older and moved away, I still had fond memories of the place in which I grew up. The more I learned the more I wanted to tell its story.

Hence this book.

This book could not have happened without the generosity of people like Marshall Sewell, Verna Thomas, Leo Whalen, Gladys

Prosperi, Aurora Semple, John Iannaccone, Larrabee C. Lillie and many others I've surely overlooked, all of whom graciously lent me their time, ears, and memories. They shared their stories with me when this book was but a whisper in the back of my mind. For that I am grateful. They taught me something very important: the greatest storehouse of knowledge of the past comes not from books, but from those who *lived* it.

The bulk of the interviews for this book, which began life as a series of articles for *The Manchester Times*, were conducted ten years ago. Sadly, some of those folks have passed on since I first began this project. Hopefully this book will help preserve some of their wit, wisdom, and memories.

I would be remiss if I did not mention those who did the heavy lifting, cataloging the past so that people like me could come along, bring it all together, and turn it into the narrative you now hold. People like William S. Dewey, John McPhee, Kevin Pace, Ronald Montgomery, Rick Zitarosa, Barbara Solem-Stull, William McMahon, Henry Charles Beck and many others are true historians. They are caretakers of a past we ought not forget. If you enjoy this book, I strongly urge you to read the works listed in the back of this volume. There you'll find a treasure trove of New Jersey history. You'll want to read every one.

And of course there is the Lakehurst Historical Society (www.lakehurstnj.org) and Navy Lakehurst Historical Society (www.nlhs.com), both of which lent me their time, expertise, and archives. Both deserve a visit, either online or in person.

Finally, I have to offer my thanks to Stewart Swann and Robyn Weber, owners of *The Manchester Times*. They gave me my first opportunity to write professionally and indulged me when I decided to tackle this crazy project. Linda Siemon and Noel Hunter also deserve thanks for looking over the manuscript and making sure I crossed all my T's. Last, but certainly not least, I have to express my sincere appreciation for all the people who read and enjoyed my original series of stories in the *Times*. You made me realize that people really do thirst for stories like this.

Thanks for reading.

Eric San Juan, 2011

LAKEHURST:
AN INTRODUCTION

For a town so rich in history, Lakehurst is embarrassingly easy to miss. Chances are if you've spent a fair amount of time in Ocean County, you've passed through town. You may not have realized you were doing so – many don't – that's how small it is. Just under one square mile, it is a small borough set right in the middle of Manchester Township; the hole in Manchester's donut. The adjacent naval base is named for Lakehurst, but even that is just beyond the town's reach, resting instead in Manchester and Jackson townships. For those driving along Route 70, maybe driving to Toms River for some shopping or to the Jersey Shore to soak up some sun, Lakehurst might seem like little more than just another small New Jersey town, forgotten as quickly as it takes to drive through.

But the borough's small size belies its rich and interesting history. A history that, surprisingly enough, helped shape the entire region in ways great and small.

That's right. Lakehurst is more than blimps.

The Hindenburg disaster, which unfolded over town in 1937, leaving 36 dead, is unquestionably the best-known piece of Lakehurst history, so much so it's now part of pop culture. A photo of the burning zeppelin graces the cover of legendary rock and roll band Led Zeppelin's first album. Jokes referring to the disaster have been on hugely popular shows like The Simpsons. The disaster has even been mentioned in a Johnny Carson monologue. Yet as we'll explore within this volume, the Hindenburg is just one of many stories to be told about this small town.

Though it had been a thriving community for many years prior, the Borough of Lakehurst was incorporated as an official municipality relatively recently, branching off on its own in 1921. It had been called the Village of Manchester, and it was during that earlier period that it helped change regional history.

Appropriately, 1921 is the same year the Lakehurst Naval Air Station was officially commissioned, arguably the starting point of Lakehurst's modern era. From 1921 to today, this facility has been a major player in Naval operations. From the development of the airship to the first helicopter squadrons to today's state-of-the-art aircraft carrier technology, Navy Lakehurst has had its hands in a great deal.

The coinciding of those events in 1921 is an appropriate quirk of history because no examination of Lakehurst would be complete without including the Navy base that shares its name — even though not a single acre of the base actually lies within the borough. Yet you simply can't tell the story of Lakehurst without telling the story of the base. The two are forever intertwined.

The earliest roots of Lakehurst date to the American Revolution. In time, industry took hold, people came, and this tiny corner of the Pine Barrens became a surprisingly active place. A town was born. With the town came more people, more industry, and a visionary named William Torrey, who would pursue dreams of a railroad empire, and in doing so would alter the face of the region forever.

Something to keep in mind as we explore the early history of Lakehurst: The name "Lakehurst" did not appear until around the turn of the 19th Century. Prior to that, Lakehurst was the Village of Manchester. Even when the name first appeared, it did so only in an unofficial capacity until the borough's true birth in 1921. Because of that, in many ways this book chronicles the early days of Manchester, too.

In the years leading up to its incorporation, Lakehurst was home to various lodges (at least one circa the 1870s that still stands to this day), a rope mill, an iron forge that made cannonballs for the Continental Army, an elite French girls school, and a Russian Embassy, among other places of note. There were also major railroad facilities, luxurious resorts, and of course, a slew of lighter-than-air airships cruising over the Lakehurst skies.

Part of the fun in mining this mountain of yesterday is that much of that history is still here for our examination. There are many pieces of Lakehurst's past that still stand. Within the pages of this book, we will not only recount some of Lakehurst's most notable stories, but we'll point readers to the people and places that can help this history come alive. Standing downtown on Union Avenue seems pretty pedestrian -- that is, until you're able to truly *see*. In reading the stories contained herein, your eyes will see the town in ways you never before imagined. You'll see steam trains and factories; immigrant rail workers and old general stores. You'll connect yesterday to today.

Of course, some stories can only be told by the people who lived them. You won't find their tales in the history books, or in pamphlets, or in the library. You'll only find them by talking to the eyes and ears of the past. Their stories are countless; ten volumes could not contain them all; but hopefully, what is presented here will offer readers a taste of what life was like in a small Pine Barrens community. Because at the end of the day, after all the facts and figures and dates and names and numbers, Lakehurst's story -- *any* town's story -- is the story of the people who lived there.

This town's story began with a furnace.

The tiny Borough of Lakehurst is located where NJ State Routes 70 and 37 meet

THE FEDERAL FORGE
AND EARLY LAKEHURST

On paper, the roots of Lakehurst do not appear to delve too deeply into the past. Incorporated as a municipality in 1921, as of this writing the town has yet to celebrate its 100th anniversary. Yet that is only a small part of the story. In truth, one would have to trace back some 250 years of history to find the roots of the Lakehurst we know today.

The first European settlement of the Lakehurst and Manchester area appears to have taken place around the 1750s, a period when pre-Revolution Americans eyed up the Pines Barrens' rich timber and water resources. There was money to be made in the vast expanse of pines that dominate the southern stretches of New Jersey, and where there was money to be made, there came settlers. Hardy, enterprising settlers – the Pine Barrens were an unforgiving, desolate place, after all, where fortunes were pulled kicking and screaming from the very earth beneath their feet. But fortunes were indeed made. As took place throughout what we now call Ocean County (and beyond), early sawmills brought people to the area seeking work.

And what a people they were. The first Pine Barrens settlers were a motley group of outcasts, runaways, those fleeing the eyes of authority, and other such people on the fringe. During the American Revolution, those disinclined to support the cause of the Revolution often found themselves in the deep places of the Jersey pines. "People with names like Britton and Brower, loyal to the King, and sometimes covered with feathers and tar, left their homes in Colonial cities and took refuge in the Pine Barrens," John McPhee wrote in his classic look at the region, *The Pine Barrens*. Quakers found themselves in the pines, too, as did Hessian deserters from the British Army.

The lumber industry was the first to gain a foothold in the Pine Barrens. Small villages, little more than worker camps, really, sprang up one after another. The land was remote and the work hard, but the income was reasonable enough for people to have made the effort to tame the Pine Barrens. The oaks of the area were cut for shipbuilding; the cedar trees for roof shingles and other construction needs; and the pines that most dominate the swath of green that still covers much of New Jersey were turned into the charcoal vital to the forges and furnaces that would come to be so important to the region's embryonic economy.

The entire immediate area surrounding Lakehurst was dotted with sawmills. In 1749, a man by the name of Mat Vanhorne, or Van Horn, according to some accounts, operated two mills in the area. One was located in Manchester, in the area now known as Whiting, the other in present day Berkeley. Another mill called Schenck's Saw Mill, named after owner Abram Shenck, was located in the vicinity of present day Cedar Glen Homes on Route 571 in Manchester. There was probably at least one more in that area, too, called the Ridgeway Mill. The sawmill at Lakehurst appears to have been attached to a later, more successful industry — ironworks.

And really, it was a natural for the next step of Pine Barrens growth. In Lakehurst — still some 100 years away from actually being *called* Lakehurst — the natural features of the Barrens were conducive to the Revolution era industries taking root in Central Jersey.

But first they had to create a lake.

The borough may now be called Lakehurst, but there is no Lake Hurst. The body of water off what is now Union Avenue is called Lake Horicon. "Horicon," the original name of New York's Lake George, derives from an Indian word meaning "silvery waters." An odd choice, since like most bodies of freshwater in the Pine Barrens the lake's cedar waters are actually a rich reddish-brown in color. The name was probably borrowed from the Horicon rook, aka Hurricane Brook, a tributary of the Toms River that feeds the lake.

Prior to 1825, the lake was called Congress Pond, and according to some accounts, it was named Federal Pond following the drafting of the United States Constitution, a patriotic but ultimately temporary name change. Up until at least 1825, it was called Manchester Pond, according to a 1908 pamphlet by Frederic C. Torrey. By In 1841, it was renamed Manchester Pond, and was ultimately named Lake Horicon in 1866 by General John S. Schultze.

Interestingly, that body of water is not of nature's making. The 60-acre lake is manmade, created when Horicon Brook was dammed in the latter portions of the 1700s. The brook was dammed with a purpose in mind.

Industry was about to arrive.

Lake Horicon was created to provide water power for what would be Lakehurst's first major industry – a forge and furnace, built to take advantage of the area's plentiful bog iron.

Bog iron is usually found in peat bogs, the result of dissolved iron being carried downstream and deposited in acidic bog environments. Early settlers pulled back layers of peat and harvested the deposited iron beneath, usually found in pea-sized nodules. Because bog iron is renewable – every 30 years or so, a spent bog can be reharvested – settlements frequently sprang up around usable bogs. Such was the case in the Pine Barrens, a landscape that was dotted with dozens of tiny villages, most now lost to time. McPhee called them "small, recursive Pittsburghs, in every part of the forest, where fine grades of pig and wrought iron were made."

A chunk of bog iron
Photo by Tomasz Kuran

The ore is far from a regional phenomenon. Bog iron has a long history on the North American continent. A thousand years of history, in fact. Evidence shows that 1,000 years ago, Norsemen in L'Anse aux Meadows, an early settlement in New Foundland, Canada, smelted bog iron for rivets and tools.

In the Pine Barrens, bog iron, along with timber, became one of the earliest and most profitable resources available. So Lakehurst, and indeed all of the Pine Barrens, were following a proud tradition.

Enter the Wright's Forge – and Lakehurst's earliest settlement roots with it.

Constructed circa 1789 by Caleb Ivins and British loyalist David Wright, the Federal Forge and Furnace was Ocean County's first such forge. (As noted, it was not uncommon for British loyalists to have settled in the Pine Barrens, where the relative

14

isolation and rich resources of the region could provide a prosperous, if quiet and unassuming, life).

It was around the forge, located roughly east of Lake Horicon and south of Church Street, near the old cemetery, that the area first grew as an industrial center.

The forge required workers, of course. After all, somebody had to mine the stuff. There were no superhighways in the 1700s and 1800s, and people did not commute to their jobs. The very idea was unheard of – and all but impossible. That meant workers had to live where they worked, especially in the remote Pine Barrens. Ivins and Wright built more than a dozen log dwellings near the forge to house workers. It became something of an embryonic Lakehurst, huddled around the foot of the lake.

"Besides the forge itself there was on the tract a good sawmill with two saws, fourteen or fifteen log dwelling houses for the workmen, a two-story frame house for the owner or manager together with other buildings suitable for storehouses, coal houses and stabling," Charles S. Boyer wrote in his 1931 book, *Early Forges and Furnaces in New Jersey.*

Such worker villages were common at the time. At least 17 forges operated in the Pine Barrens during the late 1700s and into the 1800s. Workers suffered through 12-hour days and seven-day weeks, working from the spring until the ponds and waterways so vital to the industry froze in late winter.

"There were no days off," McPhee wrote, "and the happiest day of the year was the day the furnace went out of blast."

For some 10 months out of the year, charcoal made from area pines, as many as one thousand acres worth of trees a year, kept the fires blasting. Seashells were hauled in from the shore to be used as flux. Deposits of old shells can still be found in the woods surrounding Lakehurst, including once plentiful piles in the woods off present day Division Avenue.

It wasn't an easy life. Among the workers, drinking was common. Life was hard. Most workers weren't even paid in United States currency, instead paid with local scripts that could only be used in company-run stores.

"The workers, often in debt to the company store long before payday arrived, found themselves continually indebted and dependant on the company," Barbara Solem-Stull wrote in *Ghost Towns and Other Quirky Places in the New Jersey Pine Barrens.*

At some forge sites, the company store manager kept a list of the employees, with notes on who was and was not to be trusted with credit based on observed character traits. One too many nights of hard drinking, which meant the next day would be less than productive, meant no credit. Break something on the job or ruin goods being produced and it came out of your pay.

"I owe my soul to the company store," sang Tennessee Ernie Ford. And sometimes it was almost the truth.

But they persevered, and the industry thrived. Wright's Forge was among those successes. Some tales say iron mined in Lakehurst was used to create cannonballs for the Continental Army, the most noteworthy in a wide range of uses. Iron from the pines was used to make cannonballs for the army at Valley Forge, and was used to create shot during the War of 1812, and was forged into the cylinders for some of the first experimental steam engines, and much more.

In Lakehurst, the forge did well enough that it was sold in 1793 to John Godfrey of Philadelphia, who changed its name to Federal Forge and erected a second furnace calling it Federal Furnace. Federal Furnace was built around 1795. Its exact location remains unclear, but in *Early Manchester and William Torrey*, William S. Dewey speculates, "We have to conclude that it must have been situated on the sloping ground on the north side of Horicon Brook ... Such an arrangement would place the furnace and forge in close proximity to one another."

Dewey also notes that there was once a pond next to Lake Horicon, on the east side of present day Lake Street. "The pond was several hundred feet long," he wrote, "with a dam at the easterly end, perhaps one quarter of the way toward Brook Street. The impounded water was run off via a sluiceway to operate blowers at the forge." The site of the pond is now swampland.

Two decades later, the forge would again change hands. In 1815, Godfrey sold out to John Clark of Philadelphia, who changed the name to Dover Forge and quickly turned it over to Griffith Jones and Isaiah Holmes. Later that same year Holmes sold his share, leaving Jones as the sole owner.

Several years later, in 1820, the site changed hands again when General Samuel J. Read took possession, changing its name to Dover Furnace. (Or, confusing records indicate, it may have been called either "Lower Forge" or "Martha Forge." Martha Forge was, in fact, a separate business altogether, located roughly in the area of present day Manchester Town Hall. In any case, the history of place names in the area is confusing and unclear, and this author is ill-equipped to sort out this particular tangled knot.

Read died in 1836. Benjamin B. Howell took possession of the property, and then his sons, Henry W. and Lewis Howell.

Remnants of the forge may still exist today. In 1908, Frederic Torrey wrote that "the remains of the old furnace were on the ground as late as 1866, and parts of the hearth stones are said to be there still. Between the house and furnace there existed in 1840 ruins of an old stamp mill where the bog iron ore was broken for the furnace." According to the National Register of Historic Places, "While the ruins have never been systematically surveyed, historian Charles Boyer reported that they were still visible in the 1920s, which would lead to the glad conclusion that they remain intact today."

Sadly, the site has never been fully explored or excavated.

In addition to cannonballs and other iron relics from the era, remnants of forges like this one can be found in some unusual places. How unusual? *Graveyard* unusual. "At some point in the early nineteenth century an industrious iron worker in the Pine Barrens decided to make a cast iron gravemarker," reports author Richard F. Vei in his book, *New Jersey Cemeteries and Tombstones: History in the Landscape.*

That's right, metal gravemarkers made of bog iron. This sort of monument "reflects the locations of the state's nineteenth-century ironworks. Some of these markers were probably expedient memorials produced because professionally carved gravestones were expensive to purchase and erect," Vei wrote. Most were produced between 1810 and 1840. Only about 40 are known to survive, none in Ocean County.

The early mining efforts of Ivins and Wright put in place the foundation upon which Manchester and Lakehurst would be built. In fact, the founding of the forge was not David Wright's only claim to local fame. It was his son, Samuel Wright, who chose the name "Manchester" for the village that would later become Lakehurst. "Manchester" was a nod to their British roots, and in 1841, the town that would later become Lakehurst was officially dubbed the Village of Manchester. It was then just a section of Dover Township but quickly developing an identity of its own.

Yet despite this, it is the name "Torrey" and not "Wright" or "Ivins" that is most associated with the early history of Lakehurst and Manchester. And there is a reason for that.

While bog iron naturally replenishes itself, like many others the Federal Forge mined the iron too quickly. "The greed of civilization has always been at the door of the Barrens," William McMahon wrote in *Pine Barrens Legends & Lore*. By the time a generation or so had passed the bog iron of the area was all but exhausted. Other regional forges shared the same fate, leading to the near wholesale collapse of the bog iron industry, and in turn the closely related charcoal industry.

Leading into the years shortly prior to the Civil War, Ocean County was experiencing prosperity enough for it to secede from Monmouth County. Yet amid this prosperity, Manchester, and in fact the entire Pine Barrens region, was flailing. In Henry Charlton Beck's regional classic, *Forgotten Towns of Southern New Jersey*, he discusses old timers circa the 1930s who "talk of old times in towns that have 'grown down' while the world was growing up."

The bog iron had run dry.

Without work, there were no workers. And without workers, there were no people.

"As the last of the iron furnaces gradually blew out and the substitute industries failed, people either left the pines or began to lead self-sufficient backwoods lives," McPhee wrote, "and while the rest of the State of New Jersey developed toward its Twentieth Century aspect, the Pine Barrens all but returned to their pre-Colonial desolation, becoming, as they have remained, a distinct and separate world."

Business was dying. People were leaving. And finally, in 1855, production at the forges and furnaces of Lakehurst ceased altogether. By the 1850s, "most of the houses in Manchester were empty," according to Harold F. Wilson's *The Jersey Shore*.

But soon, a man named Torrey – thanks in part to a wedding gift – would help reverse the souring fortunes of the Village of Manchester.

WILLIAM TORREY, KING OF THE PINES

The Village of Manchester was in a time of transition. The forge and furnace around which the first European settlements sprang was in its final years, its embers cooling, and ultimately, dying.

As the fortunes of the Federal Forge waned, the future of the village may have seemed bleak. Yet there was hope. The first glimmer of that hope came, strangely enough, with a wedding.

One hundred years prior to Lakehurst's incorporation as an officially recognized municipality, the area that would become a borough was given to a young couple as a wedding gift. That gift was the seeds of what would be a new start for the village, a time of brief but fantastic renewal for a bog iron town that had outlived its usefulness. Into this tale of gifts and new beginnings comes the name William S. Torrey, well known as the founder of the Village of Manchester.

Born in 1797, according to the Torrey Family Genealogy (his monument at the Church Street graveyard claims 1798), Torrey was the third child of a William Torrey, a Captain in the Continental Army, and later owner of William Torrey and Company in 1796 on Pearl Street in New York City. He would grow up to become a Pine Barrens railroad baron, and in doing so would change the course of not just Lakehurst history, but the history of the State of New Jersey.

Somewhere along the line, William Torrey met Adeline Whittemore. She was the daughter of a New York City banker, Samuel Whittemore, president of Greenwich Bank. William and Adeline fell in love, and on April 18, 1821, they were married. For their marriage, Adeline's father gave his daughter a gift — just over a square-mile of land. It was "land in the undeveloped and almost inaccessible region centering in what is now Lakehurst."

The gift may not have been a happy one for Mr. Whittemore. According to an historic sites survey conducted in the early 1980s by the Ocean County Cultural and Heritage Commission, "It is said that Mr. Whittmore disapproved of his daughter's marriage ... the Manchester purchase is said to have been made in her name, rather than by or for her husband."

Yet tradition being what it is, the gift was given. The stage was now set for change. With that wedding gift, the Village of Manchester's second era began in earnest.

Change did not happen right away. In fact, the newlyweds would not set foot on their new land for some two more decades. After their marriage, William and Adeline kept busy having kids, ten in all while living in New York. Samuel was the first, born in 1823; Anna the last, born 1840. An eleventh child, Lewis, was born in Manchester in 1844, but he died as an infant.

Yet soon they would come. Real estate interests probably drew them, as William had his eye on the vast swath of land – about 27,000 acres – encompassing what would eventually become the Township of Manchester. (The Village of Manchester, remember, was the early name for the tiny Borough of Lakehurst, not the name for the larger township.)

So it was that in 1841, William and Adeline took the train to Freehold, about 20 miles north of Lakehurst as the crow flies. From there it was horse and wagon through the increasingly sparse lands of central New Jersey. Their land awaited them.

First, the couple sketched out a grid of streets. William named the main streets running east and west after trees – Pine, Cedar, Maple, and so on – while Adeline named the north and south cross streets after flowers – Lilac and Rose, for example. They were so-called "paper" streets, of course, but in the years that followed they would become reality. Those street names are still used to this day. A post office was established in 1841, too. Henry J. Bulkly was the first postmaster.

The first steps toward building the Lakehurst we know today had begun. And there was more to come.

That same year, Torrey bought his 27,000 acres. For the purpose of this book we focus on Torrey's role as the founder of Lakehurst, yet in truth he was the founder of greater Manchester, in square miles one of the largest municipalities in New Jersey. His eye was aimed at creating a regional network of industry. The Torreys picked up the village's forge and furnace in the purchase, and hoped to parlay their operations into even more business. In Lakehurst, he began to manufacture charcoal. Brick kilns in which lumber was charred were located on Center Street, roughly in the area now occupied by a local restaurant on Union Avenue.

That charcoal had to go somewhere. Enter the rails.

Old Hollywood is littered with films about railroad barons building tremendous empires, men with vision that stretched beyond the horizon, willing to tame man and nature in the quest for a legacy. In some ways, Torrey was the Pine Barren equivalent, though on a much smaller scale. His ambition knew no bounds. He wanted to build a vast empire. Called by some the King of the Pines – and his faith in the rails called "childlike" by yet others – he saw railroads, sawmills, villages and forges. A small kingdom. For a time, he even managed to see some of his dream come to fruition.

It was via the rails that the most significant portions of Torrey's empire were built. His first rail line was made of wood. He experimented with a locomotive – around 1850 it went from Lakehurst Toms River – but it proved too heavy for the wooden rails and the idea was quickly abandoned. An early derailment probably did not help the cause. Instead, the rail cars were pulled by mules. Those mules hauled cars filled with charcoal to the Beachwood area, on the south side of the Toms River, where the charcoal was eventually shipped to New York. This line is credited with being the first on the Jersey Shore. Ultimately, the experiment failed. The line ceased operations in 1846. Yet with that experimental line, Torrey caught the rail bug. It was a modest start to what would be a sweeping, albeit short-lived, conquest of the pines.

Torrey's Pine Barrens railroad empire did not come easily. There were rivalries. Battles. Nearly catastrophic failures. Yet for a time ... success. Tenuous success. Shaky success. Barely-there success. But success nonetheless.

The early to middle portions of the 1800s were a difficult time for the country, as they were for the infant town of Lakehurst, then still called the Village of Manchester. The Federal Forge had faded and died, but William Torrey had come to town, and with him came renewed life. His vision of a Pine Barrens railroad empire would keep the Village of Manchester alive for several decades, guiding not just the area's industry, but the nature of day-to-day life in this small outpost in the pines.

Life in the post-Forge years leading through the Civil War and up to the turn of the century was built around Torrey's railroad. Slowly, the village began to pick itself up again, looking towards a future without bog iron.

Following the 1841 purchase of and arrival to Manchester by Torrey and his sprawling family, the village began to grow enough to become something of a center of power in the area.

The year 1850 marks one of the great turning points in regional history. That year, the southern portion of Monmouth County seceded, becoming what we know today as Ocean County. The Village of Manchester, already showing great promise as an industrial center, was a strong contender to become the seat of the newly incorporated county.

That may have been part of Torrey's grand plan; Lakehurst's Union Avenue was designed and aligned to be the main road to Toms River, then a small but key shipping center. He was clearly thinking ahead, seeing the Village as central to life in the region. An ill-fated decision made during the construction of a north-south railroad line would further cement this notion. Torrey wanted the Village of Manchester (soon to be called Lakehurst) to be a regional power.

But it was not to be.

When the time came to vote on Ocean's county seat, Lakehurst was passed over in favor of Toms River *by a single vote.*

Had the vote gone differently, Lakehurst would have been an entirely different community. Had fate dealt that hand, there is no telling what the community would look like today. Still a sleepy little borough in the pines? Maybe. Or maybe it would have turned into a boom town, drawing the wealthy and powerful, decision-makers and political players. We'll never know.

For now, the railroads beckoned.

Lakehurst is "inextricable linked to the early railroad history of southern New Jersey and therefore, by extension, to the upheavals wrought by the rails upon the region," claims a document filed with the National Register of Historic Places in 2001. "There is no other place in the entire Pinelands whose history is so dependent upon, and intertwined with, the early development of railroading ... While a number of other settlements owe their location and early prosperity to the advent of rail transportation, there is none that was founded (or, more accurately, re-founded) to be the lynchpin and focal point of a rail system."

Going into the 1850s, the New Jersey State Legislature was looking closely at the state's rail transportation system. Railroads connecting New York City and the Philadelphia area, as well as southern New Jersey and beyond, would be key to the state's continued economic development. There were already rails throughout the state, most owned by the Camden and Amboy Railroad, but there were holes in the state's infrastructure. It was here that Torrey saw his chance.

"Lack of transportation by rail into the Manchester-Toms River area had, by that time, aroused the attention of William Torrey," wrote Dewey. "Together with son John, he proposed a new line to run from Port Monmouth on Raritan Bay to Cape May via Toms River. It was planned that the road would be a link in a chain visualized to extend all the way from New York City to Norfolk, Virginia."

In 1854, Torrey managed to land himself a spot on a multi-state committee formed to examine the proposal.

Yet it was not to be. Too big a project. Too many hurdles. It died in the idea stage.

But in that same year, something else took place that would ensure Torrey got his chance to play at the railroad business. He, along with nine others from Monmouth, Burlington, Atlantic and Cape May counties, formed the Raritan and Delaware Bay Railroad Company. His son, William A. Torrey would be company secretary. Representatives of the Camden and Amboy Railroad were less than thrilled at the prospect of a competitor but, with the blessing of the legislature, a competitor is exactly what they had.

In 1855, Raritan and Delaware Bay finalized contracts to construct a railroad that would realize at least a portion of the failed dream of the year prior: a line running from Raritan Bay to Cape May. The following year, a groundbreaking took place in Port Monmouth. William A. Torrey would supervise construction; his brother, Samuel, would work with the company's finances. Hopes were high from the start.

"The advantages afforded by this road are that it opens access to a vast deal of unoccupied land," enthused the September 10, 1862 edition of the *New York Tribune*. "We have no doubt this will be not only one of the most delightful but one of the cheapest and quickest routes from New York to Philadelphia."

In fact, Torrey's ultimate vision reached even farther south than Philadelphia. He saw beyond the vast, untamed wilderness of pines between Manchester and the City of Brotherly love and envisioned a rail network that would connect much of the East Coast.

"It may have seemed unproductive to build a railroad through the undeveloped Pine Barrens in the mid-nineteenth century," wrote Lorett Treese in the 2006 book *Railroads of New Jersey: Fragments of the Past in the Garden State Landscape*, "but this railroad's promoters intended it to be part of a larger system extending from the New York to Norfolk, with ferries across the Delaware and Chesapeake bays."

Yet for all those hopes and dreams, money problems arose quickly. As the line inched its way south, construction was halted in 1857 thanks to dwindling finances. The next year, the estate of Joseph Brick, for whom Brick Township is named, invested in the project, eager to see the line reach Lakewood. The influx of cash helped, but progress remained slow. By 1861, the line had finally reached the northern borders of Ocean County.

It was in Ocean County that a mistake was made. A mistake that would all but doom the railroad.

END OF AN EMPIRE

Torrey's railroad dreams were quickly coming to fruition. The slow, steady march southward was finally falling into place. Success, it seemed, was on the horizon. But during the construction through Ocean County, a fateful decision was made.

As approved by the legislature, plans called for the line to veer from Lakewood (then called Bricksburgh) to Toms River, a small but growing village off Barnegat Bay named for the river upon which it sat. The village had played a small role in the American Revolution when on March 24, 1782 its blockhouse was attacked and taken by British forces. In 1850, it had been named seat of Ocean County. Yet Toms River was not destined for rails after all. Concerned with the economic development of Manchester, still seeing it as the center of a small industrial empire, the Torreys changed the route. The railroad would not turn towards the shore, as planned, but would instead stay about 12 miles inland and aim for the heart of the Village of Manchester. After passing through the village, they would deviate further, pushing southwest to Atsion, and hence enabling access to Camden and Philadelphia via the Camden and Atlantic Railroad. Torrey and company were now in direct competition with the Camden and Amboy rail monopoly.

They would come to regret that decision.

For now, the operation was pushing forward. On April 8, 1862, the railroad had reached the Village of Manchester. By the following year it connected with the Camden and Atlantic Railroad, at 85 miles becoming the longest line in the state. A spur was added that same year, connecting Lakehurst and Toms River.

Manchester was quickly turned into a bona fide railroad town. Maintenance shops were constructed. A roundhouse and turntable, along with machine shops and more, were built. Operations in town continued nearly 24 hours a day.

"The Railroad yard and station were busy places. There switch engine crews made up units to be picked up by the night freights and mixed cargoes were transferred to cars to be picked up by the local freights which carried them to the station to the North and down to South Jersey as far as the Delaware Bay at Bayside," wrote Frank Wainwright in a 1971 edition of the *Advance Nickel News*, a small newspaper once published in Manchester. (Longtime residents will remember the *Advance* as at one time the voice of the area, a two-section local newspaper named after its price that covered all things Manchester and Lakehurst. After a long decline, including the deaths of both its founder, Thomas Varelli, and his son, the paper folded in the 2000s.)

Torrey, it should be noted, was not focused solely on this one matter. In the 1850s, he helped establish churches in Toms River, in 1862 founded the Alliance Steamboat Company with his brother, Joseph, and sons William A. and Samuel, in 1866 started a brickyard in the Whiting section of Manchester, among other endeavors. Real estate. New business. Building community. Torrey dabbled in it all.

Yet most of all, Torrey had visions of railroads to pursue.

The intent was in part to utilize the railroad for tourism (though there is some historical question as to whether Torrey envisioned tourism as central to the village's future). The Raritan and Delaware Bay Railroad was well positioned to do exactly that, unifying the northern and southern parts of the state and providing a rail link between New York and Philadelphia. An 1861 newspaper account gushed, "ten thousand streams of prosperity, wealth, joy and happiness will flow, irrigating and radiating every part of our new county!!" The writer was less than prophetic. During the Civil War years, most of the people transported along the rail line were anything but tourists. They were soldiers fighting the War Between the States.

"The outbreak of the Civil War marked the most prosperous period of the Raritan & Delaware Bay Railroad's existence," a late 1800s newspaper indicated. "All the transportation of troops from New York and New England had been by the Camden and Amboy until it appeared that some of the management of that road were not heartily in favor of putting down the rebellion."

The Camden and Amboy was accused of being slow to transport troops on their way to the battles of the south. The Raritan & Delaware, however, favored Union troops with speedy transportation. When the President Abraham Lincoln placed all railroads under the control of the government on May 25, 1862, the Raritan was the New Jersey line that benefited most.

Yet the revenue generated by the war was short-lived; mercifully for the country at–large, but near-disastrously for Torrey and his railroad company.

"Torrey's profits were not outstanding," a 1981 county Historical Survey indicates. "The railroad did, however, open the area for settlement."

Much of that settlement came as part of the railroad's operations. But it stayed and helped build a community. The Village of Manchester had now completely left the days of the Forge behind. It was becoming a new community; a small but vital community made up of hard-working, poor immigrants looking to carve out their own piece of Americana from the empty Pine Barrens.

In the 1860s, workers from England and Ireland were brought to Lakehurst to work on the rails. They were promised decent wages and food. More importantly, they were provided a place to call their own. Many of those workers lived along Hibernia Avenue, a one-block stretch of road few outside of town ever see. Linking Route 70 and Center Street, the avenue offers a hazy glimpse into Lakehurst's railroading past. Many of the homes there are the same cottages built around the 1880s for the borough's Irish railroad workers.

If there was a time for the Village of Manchester to become a town of its own, it was now. Torrey wanted it. If he was going to see Manchester turn into a bona fide industrial center, he *needed* it. On April 6, 1865, it happened. Manchester would no longer be merely a place within Dover Township. It would be a town of its own. All 84 square miles of it, including the tiny village at the center of it all.

Lakehurst, however, remained the Village of Manchester, one part of a much larger town. Lakehurst would not be incorporated as an independent municipality for another 56 years. Only Pine Beach (1925), Ship Bottom (1925), South Toms River (1927), and Barnegat Light Borough (1948) are "younger" than Lakehurst as far as being officially recognized as an Ocean County municipality. Despite this, the small town was quickly developing a personality of its own. Though Lakehurst and Manchester were founded at the same time by the same person, over the years

Lakehurst would find itself becoming distinctly separate from Manchester.

But for the moment, Lakehurst was little more than downtown Manchester.

It was not a huge village – the year Manchester was incorporated, the population was a meager 1,054 – but prospects looked good. "The village at present is one of railroad workshops with neat cottage residences for the workers, a church and schoolhouse, two or three stores and as many taverns," historians John N. Barber and Henry Howe declared in their 1868 volume, *Historical Collections of the State of New Jersey.*

On the surface, things appeared to be going well in the Village of Manchester. But like the Federal Forge decades prior, the end of this short stretch of thriving years was in sight.

"Economic disaster," Dewey wrote, "would not be long in overtaking the Torrey family's railroad empire."

There were warning signs as early as 1863. William A. Torrey stepped down from the railroad's board of directors. Cash flow continued to be an issue. That same year, the Torrey family was forced to sell 25,000 of their 27,000 acres in order to keep the dream alive. And worse yet, rivals intent on seeing the end of the Raritan and Delaware Bay still watched, and waited, and plotted, and planned. The Camden and Amboy Railroad had never forgiven the Raritan and Delaware Bay for encroaching on its turf.

The Torreys' decision to reroute the line through their growing village, and hence allow passenger rails to compete directly with the Camden and Amboy Railroad, was about to come back to haunt them.

From the moment Torrey's line began operation, his competitors filed suit. The Camden and Amboy charged that by altering its route, the Raritan and Delaware had violated its charter. The lawsuit was a financial drain on the Raritan and Delaware. In November 1867, the Appellate Court agreed. Deviating from the route, and hence its charter specifications, had made Torrey's railroad a "wrongdoer." Worse still, the mounting financial problems meant the company could not pay its many debtors.

That was the end of the Raritan and Delaware Bay Railroad.

It's fascinating to speculate what would have been had the original route been followed. Instead of a rail line passing through a growing but otherwise unremarkable rail village, continuing south through the vast expanse of the Pine Barrens, it would have journeyed closer to the Jersey Shore, into a new and vibrant county seat, and through areas that could have made it a vital means of transportation for the entire state.

"Had it been built as at first announced," Dewey wrote, "near the coastline where old and populous villages were already located and where access to harbors and rivers and mill-seats would have made it available as a means of traffic as well as travel, its operation would have been attended with larger success, the opposition which it aroused from the Camden and Amboy Company, on account of its endeavoring to be a competing road, would never have arisen, and thousands of dollars ... would have been saved."

Dewey argued that the decision to alter the line's course "retarded the development of the shore region for many years." And he's probably right. Passing as far inland as it did, Torrey's rail line offered little to New Jersey industry and even less to New Jersey passengers.

By 1870, the company was reorganized under financier Jay Gould and its assets were taken over by the New Jersey Southern Railroad. Even that wouldn't last. The rails suffered blow after blow. A sharp economic downturn called the Panic of 1873 forced the railroad into bankruptcy. It reopened in 1874, but again went bankrupt in 1879. The Central Railroad of New Jersey finally took over. The Torreys were out of the picture.

The dream was dead.

When the railroad appeared ready to fade from sight, Torrey did exactly that. He left town in 1865 and moved to Montclair. He was 68. Much of his family would stay – historical maps of the borough are littered with the term "Torrey house," indicating homes belonging to the family – and would continue to play a vital role in the development of Lakehurst for decades to come.

Adeline Torrey died on October 9, 1890. She was buried in Lakehurst's old Presbyterian Cemetery on Church Street, the all-but-invisible Victorian avenue (despite once being the main road to Toms River) running parallel to Union Avenue near Lake Horicon.

William Torrey returned to find a changing Lakehurst. On June 15, 1891, now in his 90s, he passed away. He, too, was buried in the Presbyterian Cemetery, resting quietly in the small town he helped put on the map. There, crumbling old gravestones, many unreadable, still bear the name of "Torrey."

He did not leave an empire, but he did leave his mark, both regionally and locally. The network of rails throughout south Jersey he helped create connected the region to the rest of the world, allowing Pine Barrens industries to flourish in a way they never could before. Local agriculture and industries like clay works, charcoal, glass, and even tourism kept parts of the Pines alive while those far removed from the rails withered and died.

And, of course, there was the mark Torrey and sons left on Lakehurst.

"Were it not for his direction," suggests a 2001 filing with the National Register of Historic Places, "Lakehurst would in all likelihood be today what other iron communities of the Pines, such as Martha and Speedwell, are – only memories and barely discernable scars deep in the pine woods."

LARRABEES,
LONGCHAMPS &
LABORERS

For a time, William Torrey was Manchester, and Manchester was William Torrey. For both good and ill, he and his family directly and indisputably guided the very nature of the area. Even beyond the borders of Manchester, his presence was a big one.

But even the good fortunes of William Torrey could not last forever. The Torrey's could not control all ends. Lakehurst would soon be forced to once again shift focus, and to build a new life. Not a life without Torreys – sons William A., Samuel, and John remained heavily involved in township affairs – but a new life nonetheless. A life on terms dictated by the people whose sweat built the town in which they lived.

Following the turbulent times of the Civil War, Lakehurst's future rested on the railroad and the work, commerce, and residents it would bring to town. What seemed to be the end of the Torrey railroad empire may have spelled the end to those good fortunes – but hard work, fate, and changing times helped Lakehurst weather the storm.

Even after the Raritan and Delaware Bay Railroad was dissolved in 1867, the railroad remained an important part of the Village of Manchester. (It would be during this period that the name "Lakehurst" would first appear, used in an unofficial capacity to describe Manchester's small downtown). The railroad continued to provide jobs, bring people to town, and serve as a focal point for the still-growing community.

Central to life in Lakehurst during this period was the Larrabee Store. Initially called the Torrey Store, it changed names in the 1860s when Edward Larrabee Sr. took over operations. For a time, the Larrabee Store was the only general store for miles – the nearest was Christopherson's in Whiting, a long trek by horse and wagon – making it an essential ingredient to life in the village. All manner of goods were available in here, serving the day-to-day needs of the Pine Barrens community. Basic tools; food; other goods. Likely, it was near impossible to thrive in Lakehurst without soliciting the shop. Larrabee's accepted an in-house script, issued by William A. and Samuel Torrey. In denominations ranging from five cents to five dollars, residents who accepted the script – often railroad workers – could spend it at the store rather than U.S. currency. Presumably, this was a boon to the Torrey's during the tough financial times of the 1860s.

To this day, the Larrabee Store is still in downtown Lakehurst. Located on the corner of Union Avenue and Locust Street, the three-story brick building is in the federal Register of Historical Places. It retains much of its original appearance and remains among the tallest buildings downtown, but is largely vacant. A series of shops, closed as quickly as they have opened, have occupied the first floor of the building in recent years. The upper floors have been empty for years and remain so as of this writing.

If there was a mover and shaker of note not named Torrey, Larrabee was the man.

The Larrabee Building on Union Avenue looks different today, but still stands at the corner of Union and Locust. *Photo courtesy of Lakehurst Historical Society*

The first Roman Catholic Church in Ocean County was built in Lakehurst. Today the historic church serves as the home of the Lakehurst Historical Society.

Edward Larrabee came to the Village of Manchester in 1862 at Torrey's behest, ostensibly to work for the railroad. Making his home at the bend on Church Street, he would go on to help boost the village's business community. He, along with Frederick Torrey of the famed Torrey family and A.L. LeRoy (proprietor of the Pine Tree Inn, which would be constructed in 1898 and which we'll discuss in later chapters) helped create the Lakehurst Board of Trade, an early chamber of commerce. They helped attract business to the community, probably not too difficult thanks to the railroad. Larrabee himself was a business. In addition to the store, he owned a cranberry bog and sawmill, both fairly common businesses for Pine Barren entrepreneurs. Larrabee would later go on to become an Ocean County Freeholder, serving from 1900 to 1915.

Around this time, the "ordinary folks" began to impact borough history, too.

In 1874, the Irish railroad workers who kept the Lakehurst trains running helped make Ocean County History when they built Old St. John's Church at 300 Center Street. It was the first Roman Catholic Church in the county. The very first mass at Old St. John's Church, which was built on land donated by William Torrey, was held later that year.

The original Stations of the Cross are still on display at the historic St. John's Church on Center Street, now home to the Lakehurst Historical Society

More than 125 years later, the church remains. Located just across from the longtime headquarters of the Lakehurst Volunteer Fire Department, the church now serves as the Lakehurst Historical Society Museum, a treasure trove of Lakehurst's history. Yet even as packed with historical artifacts as the church is, it retains much of its own unique history. To this day, the original Stations of the Cross still adorn the walls of the historic building, a link to worship services that took place generations ago.

The people of Lakehurst were laying down roots they would not soon shake; two other borough churches date from roughly the same period. The Old Methodist Church tucked away on Pine Street was constructed in the 1870s, while the Presbyterian Church on Orchard Street followed about three decades later in 1903.

It was also during this period that the Red Men's Lodge hall was built on Union Avenue. That building still stands, now serving as the home of the Fleet Reserve, Branch 124. Tall, white and simply adorned, the building is impossible to miss, an archaic, aged structure sleeping at the end of a business district struggling to keep up with the 21st Century. Old time residents still remember it fondly. Over the years, the lodge served as a gathering place for borough residents, offering music, dance, companionship, and more. Such places were, and remain, an integral part of small town life. They were a refuge from the daily grind of work and a retreat from what was often a hard home life. They were a place where neighbors told stories, shared news, traded gossip, and forgot their cares. Of course, by today's social standards not all was good in the Red Men's Lodge. For a time, the hall provided Village residents with a once common form of American entertainment now all but extinct: minstrel shows.

First rising to popularity in the 1830s and 1840s, minstrel shows were acts featuring white men in blackface. Dressed up as plantation slaves, they usually performed songs and dances in a parody of blacks in America. They were often mean-spirited and hateful. "Jim Crow" and "Mr. Tambo" are two of the most famous minstrel characters. The shows remained popular throughout America, especially in the South, well into the 1950s, when the politics of race in America began to change. An ugly part of our nation's history, now gone but not forgotten.

Yet not all was so base and crass. Lakehurst had a "prim and proper" side during this time, too. Late during this period, circa the 1890s, a French woman named Mademoiselle E. Debray-Longchamp founded a finishing school for girls. The school, called The Cedars (though sometimes referred to as Longchamps French School For Girls), performed the arduous task of transforming young girls into "proper ladies," teaching them manners, how to conduct themselves in a "ladylike" fashion, and generally preparing them to act as if they had stepped out of a Jane Austen novel.

Historian William S. Dewey placed the school in the area of Church and Lake streets, roughly in what is now the backyard of 310 Church Street. Its circular driveway fronted Church and Brook streets. Dewey speculates that the school may have been the mansion house of William Torrey, which itself was once the site of forge founder Caleb Wright's early home.

The building, alas, no longer exists, and no evidence remains save some old photographs. In the 1980s, however, some residents claimed to still recall the school.

The small village had its share of political big wigs, too. Well, *small time* political big wigs, at least. Circa 1908, the town still had only about 800 residents.

Frederic C. Torrey described Lakehurst in 1980 as "picturesque and forest-edged."

Where there is growth and an opportunity to make money, inevitably there is politics. In the latter portion of the 19th Century, the epicenter of politics in the Village of Manchester was Rogers Hotel, built on Union Avenue in 1884. It was named after its owner, Charles Rogers, who was a county Freeholder. Rogers Hotel wasn't as much a hotel as it was a tavern – as any longtime resident will tell you, one of many taverns that would call Lakehurst home over the years. Like so many historic places in town, the Rogers Hotel can still be seen on Union Avenue – but it's unlikely that the region's political future is still being discussed there. These days, it's an ice cream shop. You won't have to look too closely to see that it still bears the name "Charles Rogers" over its door, though.

And so it went. In many ways, it was becoming a new Lakehurst. The days of the Torrey railroad empire were fading. A new day, with an unexpected new focus, was approaching.

At The Turn Of The Century

At the turn of the century, life in the Village of Manchester revolved around the railroad – and around the railroad evolved a new industry that would for a few brief decades give the small town a new reason to be on the map, replacing the dead forge and the dying rails.

That industry? Tourism.

Even more noteworthy, it was right around this time that the name "Lakehurst" began being used in earnest. And in fact, tourism was the reason.

Though the name "Lakehurst" had been previously used in an unofficial capacity, it did not see regular use until 1897, when the "Lakehurst" designation was established at the local post office. The idea was to "increase its popularity as a winter resort." The name was prompted in part by a name change undergone by the Township of Lakewood. Once called "Bricksburgh," the name was changed to the more pastoral "Lakewood" when its resort industry began to take root, a change designed to highlight the once relaxing nature of the town. In Lakewood, the 300-room Laurel House sparked a resort renaissance in 1880. Luminaries such as Mark Twain and Rudyard Kipling stayed at the stately hotel. Others quickly followed suit, including the Hotel Carasaljo, and the sprawling Lakewood Hotel, built in 1891 and boasting "all the luxuries of the city and all of the attractions of the country" for its 700 guests.

Vacationing in central New Jersey? Yes. The region's close proximity to New York and Philadelphia meant it was not an arduous trip for those with means, while its relative seclusion offered people a chance to truly get away. John D. Rockefeller famously purchased hundreds of acres in Lakewood, building himself an escape that remains impressive to this day.

People in Lakehurst noticed. If Lakewood could play host to a resort, why not Lakehurst? It boasted a beautiful lake, swaying pines and a remote yet accessible location, after all. So plans got underway.

But first, that name ...

With the tourism industry looming on the horizon in the Village of Manchester – following the collapse of their railroad dreams, William Torrey's sons William A., Samuel, and John, saw tourism as the future for the borough – the name "Lakehurst" was finally made official. With that, tourism was on its way.

It was in 1898 that the Pine Tree Inn, which we'll discuss at length in a later chapter, first opened its doors. For just over three decades, it would be an important part of life in the borough. It would provide revenue, provide an image, and most importantly, provide jobs.

While Lakehurst's new resort persona would provide work for local residents, it wouldn't necessarily be a step up from the manual labor that ruled the day. Blue collar was the *only* collar in Lakehurst. There were, of course, scores of railroad workers. There was work in the cranberry bogs that dotted the area. And there was the rope factory.

The factory was the second largest industry in town, trailing only the railroad, and provided jobs for dozens. It was located in roughly the same area now occupied by the post office, but its exact location remains unclear. The factory's operations included one surprisingly complex feature that is likely the final trace of this once important business: An underground pipeline that ran behind Church Street, bringing water from Lake Horicon. The water was used to run the factory's water wheel, a key part of the rope-making process. Stretches of the pipeline still exist today, buried beneath the earth over the course of the hundreds of yards between the lake and the old site. We know this because every once in a while, the pipeline is "rediscovered."

"It caved in in my yard a little over a year ago," Church Street resident Larrabee C. Lillie, grandson of Edward Larrabee Sr., told this author in May 2004. "I filled it back in," he explained.

Other Church Street residents have reported 'shallow spots' in their yard, possibly from the same pipeline.

Some say that parts of the factory itself could still be found years after it was gone. "I remember as a boy seeing some remnants," Lillie told me, "but that (the factory) burned down before I was born."

Lillie is a borough old-timer, but not *that* old. The borough's now forgotten rope factory burned to the ground in March 1911. What sparked the blaze we do not know, but what we do know is that it helped see the creation of Volunteer Fire Company No. 1 (which became Lakehurst Volunteer Fire Company in 1918). They fought the blaze to no avail and the factory was lost. At its worst, reports indicate, the massive fire threatened to burn down the entire town.

Today there doesn't seem to be any trace of the old rope factory. The woods where it is said to have been are overgrown and thick with brambles and bogs, nearly impassable in places. Further, the post office and its parking lots are on some of the land that was probably home to the factory. It is likely any ruins were paved over

The Whelan Hotel, at right, once stood on Union Avenue in roughly the same location at the current headquarters of The Manchester Times, a local newspaper.

Photo courtesy of Lakehurst Historical Society

long ago. All that's left are traces of the pipeline.

At the turn of the century, Lakehurst was becoming a quiet place, no longer plagued by the constant noise of the forge and furnace. People noticed that peace, and took solace in it. Thanks to the solitude Lakehurst offered, the borough boasts a bit of literary history – easily forgotten among all the forges, trains, inns and airships associated with the town's past. In 1912, poet Austin Miles penned "In The Garden," inspired by his mother's Pine Street garden.

Shortly after Miles penned his poem, more change came to Lakehurst. This change, unlike the loss of the rope factory, was an addition rather than a subtraction.

In 1913, politics moved from the Rogers Hotel, where once the big fish of this small pond did what politicians do, to a brand new town hall. Located on Union Avenue just a few doors down from the railroad crossing, Borough Hall served as the center of Lakehurst government, and did so for many decades. Over 90 years later, however, it too will be retired; as of this writing, plans are in the works to convert the old fire company headquarters on Center Street into a new borough hall. The eventual fate of the historic borough hall remains unclear.

When politics jumped across the street to Borough Hall, so did Charles Rogers, founder of the Rogers Hotel. At least, in spirit he did. Rogers became Lakehurst's first mayor in 1921, serving until 1924. You see, Lakehurst had finally struck out on its own, seceding from Manchester Township.

Yet 1921 is a significant milestone in borough history not just because it was the year Lakehurst became a municipality of its own. It was the start of Lakehurst's modern era, and was unquestionably the beginning of a period that would once and for all put Lakehurst on the map. Shortly after rope burned, Austin Miles wrote, and politics relocated, events just outside Lakehurst's borders were falling into place that would pave the way for the biggest and most noteworthy new resident in the tiny Pine Barrens community's history.

The United States Navy.

THE RUSSIANS
COME TO TOWN

More than a century after the Manchester area was settled, first by bog iron miners and later by railroad tycoons, the small Pine Barrens village now called Lakehurst was again changing. The days of the railroad that once looked as if they would never end were destined to wane and ultimately fail – though that death would be a slow one. So, too, would Lakehurst's status as a resort town be but a short-lived chapter in Lakehurst history (as described in a later chapter).

But something more notable – and more permanent – was on its way. Something that would usher in the modern era of Lakehurst.

That something was the United States Navy. If the early-to-middle days of Lakehurst's history were defined by the railroad, it can be safely argued that the middle-to-modern days are best defined by the Naval base and the lighter-than-air vessels that famously called the base home.

And famous they were. Glorious, majestic aircraft that coasted through the skies like nothing anyone had before seen. Children, adults, young and old, once you see an airship you never forget it, and no place on Earth has ever hosted airships like Lakehurst. This is, of course, no secret. Lakehurst's ties with airships have long been common knowledge in Ocean County. The borough's links with the railroad, too, are no secret. What many don't know is that a third and far more obscure thread in Lakehurst's past links them both together. The Navy base's origins lie in this largely unknown blip in the past, a curious footnote that involved a brief period when the town found itself home to the Russian Army.

That's right. The Russian Army.

During World War I, the tiny Borough of Lakehurst (then still part of Manchester) was home to a Russian embassy, and more surprising still, barracks of Russian soldiers. The town's residents could not have foreseen it, but those Russians would play a part, however small, in a series of events leading to the creation of the Naval base, changing the face of the borough, and indeed the entire region, forever.

On a portion of land now occupied by the Naval base, in the area of the base's back gate, a subsidiary of the Baldwin Locomotive Works called the Eddystone Ammunition Corporation

This Union Avenue building has been a post office, grocery store, dance studio, and more.
Photo courtesy of Lakehurst Historical Society

began operations in 1915. Just outside of town, the corporation constructed shells for the Imperial Russian Government. The company established a proving ground on the site to test the shells, which were later shipped overseas. Inspectors for that government were on hand from 1915 to 1917, making sure the shells were up to snuff. Russian inspectors on American soil? Yes indeed. The Cold War this wasn't. And so off in the not-very-far distance, village residents would hear the dull, steady "thoomp, thoomp, thoomp" of shelling. Other weapons, including a gun used for firing "barbed-wire projectiles," were tested there as well. It was this proving ground that spawned the name Proving Ground Road, which branches off of Chestnut Street at the rear of Pinehurst Estates, the military housing community in Lakehurst, and past a series of cranberry bogs to the base's now-closed rear gate.

Also on the grounds were barracks, occupied by Russian soldiers who worked on the site. Those soldiers were anything but invisible to Lakehurst residents. The military men used to bring sheep and goats from the railroad down Union Avenue, walking them through the center of town to Proving Ground Road, and then on to their temporary American homes.

In 1917, the United States Army entered the picture, purchasing the land from the Eddystone Corporation. Out went the Russians. In came what would be called Camp Kendrick, a short-lived testing facility for chemical weapons. The camp itself was well constructed, featuring rows of barracks, utility poles, a large headquarters, and other facilities. There was even a steam locomotive to haul in supplies via spur connecting to the Central Railroad's lines. "In contrast to the doughboys in the rotting trenches of Europe, soldiers stationed at Lakehurst enjoyed steam heat, electric lights, and 'thoroughly modern latrine facilities,'" noted Kevin Pace, Ronald Montgomery, and Rick Zitarosa, historians with the Navy Lakehurst Historical Society. It was one of the army's key sites for testing chemical weapons, which would play a vital – and devastatingly inhumane – role in World War I. Live chemical weapons, including mustard gas, were tested at Camp Kendrick.

The range of scope of the testing was extensive. A system of trenches not unlike the front lines in Europe was constructed, winding here and there through clear-cut fields. Smoke bombs would be set off to test the wind. Two observation towers would gauge the wind, then call for deadly gas shells to be shot. Observations were recorded and the process began anew. Sometimes, live sheep were put in the trenches to test the effects of the gas. The results helped the military measure the effect of various exposure levels ... and we're sure the sheep were glad to help! Range officers decked out in gas masks and other protective gear were a common sight.

But soon world conditions would change, as would the needs of the military. At the end of World War I, the Lakehurst Proving Grounds at Camp Kendrick was closed. In 1923, as the last remnants of the proving grounds were being dismantled, some 120 buildings, the old barracks from the camp, were put up for sale.

To this very day, some of those barracks can still be seen in Lakehurst.

Where they *are*, however, remains partially unclear.

Shortly after operations ceased, at least seven of those barracks were sold to Lakehurst residents. In 2000, the late Verna Thomas, longtime Lakehurst resident and a key volunteer with the Lakehurst Historical Society, told this author that she almost bought one, but at the time could not come up with the $100 it would have cost to move the structure to a new location. She passed on the deal, but others bought up the buildings, got them hauled to empty lots scattered around the village, and refurbished them as homes.

A little is known about the current whereabouts of a few of the barracks, though not much in the way of specifics. Today, at least two are located on Pine Street, and another is somewhere on Lilac Street, though it's now near impossible to identify exactly which homes they are. Yet there they are, an all but invisible link to an unusual chapter in Lakehurst's past. Another piece of history (nearly) lost.

Though unusual, though all but forgotten, this brief hint of Russians and mustard gas and sheep in trenches set the stage for what is arguably the single most significant part of Lakehurst's development – the founding of the Naval Air Engineering Station, or as it is more commonly known, the Lakehurst Navy Base.

The airships were coming.

ENTER THE AIRSHIPS

While the Village of Manchester was venturing off on its own, becoming the Borough of Lakehurst, just outside the town's borders new visitors would soon arrive. Visitors that would come to define Lakehurst to this very day.

Those visitors were the airships.

The history of airships at Lakehurst is an integral part of the borough's identity, icons not just for a small New Jersey town, but for an era gone by. Airships are on the borough seal and painted on the walls of local restaurants. They appear on postcards and are stitched into commemorative blankets. Their image dots Lakehurst from end to end. Simply put, no history of Lakehurst would be complete without mentioning these majestic aircraft which, in their heyday, were routinely seen drifting through the Ocean County skies.

These days, lighter-than-air aircraft are known for hovering over sports arenas and little more. In the early days of the 20th Century, however, airships played an important role in the American military, including a key role in both world wars. Navy Lakehurst was central to it all. A testing ground. A training ground. The central location for the military's lighter-than-air operations.

But how did the airships get to Lakehurst in the first place? After all, the northern fringes of the New Jersey Pine Barrens hardly seems like an obvious location for this relatively new, largely untested military technology.

The earliest working lighter-than-air vessel in the United States was the California Arrow. Taking flight in 1903 thanks to the design efforts of Thomas S. Baldwin, the groundwork was laid for a rich, albeit brief, future for lighter-than-air flight. Early tests of the Arrow were a success. In 1908, the military entered the picture and the U.S. Army purchased an airship from Baldwin. The figurative ball was rolling. The groundwork was in place.

It's worth noting, the California Arrow was far from the first lighter-than-air flight. The first ever balloon flight was made in

France way back in 1783. Some archeologists and historians even theorize that ancient Peruvians flew in balloons hundreds of years before that, though the theory has never been proven.

It was the California Arrow, however, that pushed such aircraft into military roles in North America. As these early efforts to develop viable airships were taking place, overseas similar endeavors were being pursued. During World War I, the Germans used lighter-than-air aircraft for patrolling and light bombing with good success – they had a fleet of over 100 of them – and continued to develop their airship technology over the years. Indeed, Lakehurst may have become the unofficial airship capital of the world, but the design for many of the most famous airships to hover over the borough came from Germany. United States military officials noticed Germany's success and began more seriously developing its own airships. As those efforts became more serious, the military sought a place to centralize airship testing. So it was that at the tail end of World War I, Lakehurst would become an integral piece of the airship puzzle.

In 1918, Navy Lakehurst had not yet come to be. It was Camp Kendrick, which fell under the oversight of the newly created Chemical Warfare Service. It was, according to Pace, Montgomery and Zitarosa's *Naval Air Station, Lakehurst*, "the site of the first full-scale gas warfare experiments in the United States."

The California Arrow takes flight with the help of an engine designed by Glenn H. Curtiss, who went on to design many airship engines. *Public domain photo*

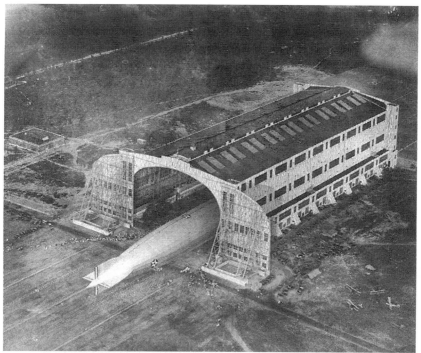

Photo # NH 44093   USS Shenandoah leaving the airship hangar at NAS Lakehurst, N.J., 1923
Photo courtesy of U.S. Naval Historical Center

But a year later, the Navy entered the picture.

In May 1919, Franklin D. Roosevelt, then Secretary of the Navy, purchased some 1,700 acres of land for use as a "dirigible field." With the potential for airships in the U.S. military looking better with each passing day, the hunt was on for sites to act as airship bases. Roosevelt thought Lakehurst fit the bill. The purchase was made for a mere $13,088. Once the land was secured, work on preparing the site began shortly thereafter. A large (and soon to be famous) project would be the centerpiece of the Navy's premier dirigible field. Hangar No. 1.

It is one of the most well-known and recognizable structures in military history, and is one of the largest of its kind, visible from miles away. At a mere 500 feet elevation, it can be seen from the oceanfront beaches of Belmar. Standing proudly off Route 547, Hangar No. 1 is the centerpiece of Navy Lakehurst. The Lord Construction Company of Philadelphia won the $2.9 million contract to construct it. It took nearly two years to complete. Measuring 966 feet by 350 feet, the hangar is 224 feet tall and capped with massive, 1,350-ton doors powered (when they were

Photo # NH 51492   USS Shenandoah flying over the New York City area, circa 1923
Photo courtesy of U.S. Naval Historical Center

fully operational) by 20-horsepower motors. For a time, it was said to be the largest manmade indoor space in the world. In 1968, it was declared a National Historic Landmark.

When the base at Lakehurst was finally commissioned on June 29, 1921 with just under 250 personnel, its most iconic structure was already in place.

It has always been impossible to grow up in Lakehurst without at least being aware of Hangar No. 1. It looms over the borough, and can be seen clearly from hilltops in Whiting. At times over the years, lucky students at Lakehurst Elementary School have been able to tour the massive gray building. At other times, it has been closed to the public. The huge doors that once housed some of the world's most famous sky-going vessels are no longer fully functional. The narrow walkways that arc some 178 feet above the heads of those on the ground are no longer safe, rickety and dangerous. The last time it held a lighter-than-air aircraft was probably the 1960s. These days Hangar No. 1 serves as a center for aircraft carrier-related training and drills, as well as office space. The interior even contains a mock aircraft carrier deck.

But as construction finished in 1921, even as the borough itself was incorporated, it quickly became a landmark, serving as the epicenter of United States airship activity.

For the next decade, things would move quickly – and tragically – in the world of airships.

In 1923, inside Hangar No. 1, the first American rigid airship was constructed, the U.S.S. Shenandoah. It was based on the designs of a German zeppelin captured during World War I. At 680 feet long, it was "the biggest thing that had ever flown in the United States," according to Pace, Montgomery, and Zitarosa. "It was also an enormous technical challenge, and navy personnel had to learn the art of flying the giant rigids." Those early tests probably made for a thrilling and sometimes dangerous time. The Navy experimented with massive mooring towers. When the great vessel was attached to such towers, windy days became an adventure. On January 16, 1924, the Shenandoah ripped free from just such a mast, tearing the airship's nose. Yet tests continued. The airship was even able to moor on masts attached to Navy ships.

Yet as would come to be learned more than once over the years, flying airships could be an all too dangerous business. In a sign of things to come, on September 3, 1925, the Shenandoah crashed over Ohio, killing 14.

Despite the crash, the American military was making great strides in rigid airship technology – but it would be the Germans who would once again send the art of airships surging forward.

Count Ferdinand von Zeppelin was a German Army officer who, after becoming enthralled with balloon flight, designed the Graf Zeppelin, the pinnacle of the rigid airships he had been designing since 1900. The 775-foot long craft, which used a rigid framework over which was stretched a cloth covering, inflated "bags" of gas within it all, was launched in 1928. It was a landmark in lighter-than-air history and would serve as the grandfather of famous airships yet to come. Luxury was the order of the day. The vehicle could accommodate twenty passengers. Gourmet meals were served on board, and a lounge area offered entertainment during trans-Atlantic flights. The Graf Zeppelin made four landings at Lakehurst, the first in 1928, making Lakehurst the first international airport in the United States. In 1929, the Graf Zeppelin circumnavigated the globe – and took just 21 days to do it. The flight helped prove that the aircraft had a place in travel.

It would be the Graf Zeppelin design that would become most famous. And infamous. You see, another airship would be based on the same design. A famous airship. A tragic airship. There are few who do not know the name "Hindenburg," the most famous Zeppelin of them all.

It would not be long before the Titanic of the Skies came to town.

But before the Hindenburg became permanently etched into the fabric of Lakehurst, that honor belonged to the sprawling and luxurious Pine Tree Inn.

TOWERS IN THE PINES

While the earliest days of Lakehurst are rooted in peat bogs and cannonballs, and later in the railroad, for a time the borough became a quiet destination for the affluent. Walking through the borough now one might never suspect that Lakehurst was once a desired vacation destination for the well to do. But it was. From 1898 to 1937, Lakehurst was home to the Pine Tree Inn, a sprawling, luxurious resort where the 'upper crust' came to find relaxation, privacy and elegance.

Lakehurst's brief tenure as a resort town came at the tail end of the village's peak years as a railroading community, with the Pine Tree Inn's construction beginning in 1895, just four years after the death of William Torrey.

"It is ironic, and perhaps fitting, that this reincarnation occurred almost simultaneously with the passing of William Torrey, who had caused the previous transformation of the dying iron settlement to a railroad town a half century earlier," a National Register of Historic Places nomination circa 2001 reads. "Again seizing on its superior railroad accessibility, Lakehurst became

Postcard courtesy of Lakehurst Historical Society

fashionable for a period."

Indeed, in 1908 Frederic Torrey wrote that "hundreds of our well-known people have acquired the 'Lakehurst-habit.'"

The draw was a sparkling lake and the quiet solitude of the Pine Barrens. What better place to escape the congestion and clamor of the city? What better way to escape from the pressing demands of business and politics? Lakehurst was accessible – William Torrey's trains saw to that – and it was *quiet.*

The famed Pine Tree Inn stood on Union Avenue, where the Lakehurst Elementary School now stands. Its bulk took up most of the block – not including the inn's tennis court, practice golf course, and two cottages across the street that housed excess guests. The whole presentation gushed luxury.

"In the heart of New Jersey's great pine forest beside beautiful Lake Horicon," proclaimed a turn of the century brochure, "surrounded on every side by pine woods, (it is) the only resort for miles around."

That wasn't strictly true, of course. Lakewood, a town blanketed by beautiful inns and hotels, was not far north of Lakehurst. But that makes the Pine Tree Inn no less impressive.

Boasting 149 rooms, the inn had five tall towers in the front, two parlors and a music room, a gift shop, a huge "amusement room" used for major events, and billiards, pool and shuffleboard rooms. Lake Horicon also featured what was in the

Sun Parlor, Pine Tree Inn, Lakehurst, N. J.

Postcard courtesy of Lakehurst Historical Society

1930s fondly called "the kissing bridge," a favorite locale for Pine Tree Inn guests. Guests even got the kind of state-of-the-art technology only the elite could enjoy in the early 1900s: steam heat and electric lighting. Even the Laurel Cottage, a side attraction that is now a wonderful old home as of this writing owned by a former mayor, boasted at the time that it was "lighted by electricity and heated by hot air furnace." Visitors to Lakehurst's premier destination enjoyed all those luxuries in an elegantly decorated facility with high-class service. The price? A mere $16 to $35 a week. That's roughly $332 to $730 in today's dollars, a bargain by any measure.

The Pine Tree Inn did not stand alone, either. A number of cottages and secondary structures served the resort, as both room for excess guests as well as housing for workers. One such cottage, the Laurel Cottage, still sits across the street from Lakehurst Elementary School.

The lake that had once been the focal point for a loud, hot, sweaty industry had now become the focal point for something much more serene.

From music to walks along the lake to quiet reading to dancing, between the late 1890s to the early 1930s the Pine Tree Inn was a prime destination, a relaxing place for a quiet getaway. The clientele of the Pine Tree Inn was, according to an early brochure, "Just a congenial family of real folks who enjoy getting away from the distractions of the cities for a day, a week-end, a week or all winter." The Pine Tree Inn was open each year from October to May, drawing "prominent folk ... here to escape for a time the high nervous strain of their occupations. Lawyers, preachers, public speakers, (and) educators find the difficult sermon or speech easier to write when nothing will disturb their quiet flow of thought."

Lakehurst's foray into hosting a resort facility followed Lakewood's lead. Lakewood boasted guests and part-time residents of great prestige, including John D. Rockefeller, George J. Gould, President Theodore Roosevelt, Mark Twain and F. Scott Fitzgerald. But a New Jersey Historical Sites Survey from 1981 claims that the Pine Tree Inn "is reputed to have had more prestigious guests than could be boasted in Lakewood; its facilities were said to be more wholesome (even having been recommended by Dr. Parkhurst, a fashionable advocate of good health)."

Who those prestigious guests were remains unclear. What is clear, however, is that whoever they were, the guests enjoyed a luxurious stay in Lakehurst. The "Dr. Parkhurst" is likely a reference to clergyman and social reformer Charles Henry Parkhurst, one of the men responsible for helping bring down New York's corrupt Tammany Hall organization of the 19th Century. Around the turn of the century he wrote in *The Christian Work* that everyone needs a quiet place to get away to replenish their sense of well-being, and that "I know of no place that will serve this purpose more admirably than 'Pine Tree Inn,' Lakehurst, New Jersey. The hotel is quiet, restful, the perfection of hospitality, and in every way delightful."

Today, the Pine Tree Inn is gone, but not forgotten. Area old-timers still have fond memories of the prestigious locale.

In the late 1930s and early 1940s, Marshall Sewell, a resident of the Crestwood section of Whiting when he was interviewed in 2004, was a reporter for the *Lakewood Daily Times* and later the *Asbury Park Press*. Before that, Sewell had ties to this key Lakehurst landmark. He moonlighted as a piano player at the Pine Tree Inn during the Great Depression.

Sewell played for Lou Pulcrano's band, which operated out of Lakewood. He would substitute for Pulcrano's sister, Dorothy, when she was not available to play. (Now Dorothy Hughes of Jackson Township, she continued to play piano at local nursing homes and senior villages for another 70 years). Playing piano at the famous inn was not a bad gig; with the luxury the Pine Tree Inn was known for, how could it be? Sewell told this author he enjoyed playing at the Pine Tree because the dance hall was just a short walk from Lake Horicon, where the band would go to relax during breaks in the music.

Though the Pine Tree Inn served as a destination for people far beyond the cozy confines of Lakehurst's borders – it was and remains a working-class, blue-collar town through and through; such luxury was beyond the means of most residents – locals sometimes got involved in the fun, too. Sewell recalled one such occasion when the inn's dance hall was livened up by the intervention of some of Lakehurst's more mischievous residents.

"One hot Fourth of July night, the windows were open in the non-air-conditioned building," Sewell recalled, "and some local boys started throwing lighted fire crackers on to the dance floor as the young women screamed."

"The manager and a local police officer were able to discourage the boys, and everything returned to normal," Sewell noted.

Times were good in Lakehurst. Some might say Norman Rockwell would have found plenty of material to work with in the tiny Pine Barrens community.

While the Pine Tree Inn was experiencing the peak of its days as a resort destination – the figurative calm before the storm of its closing – Lakehurst's famous airships were also in the midst of their glory days. Glory days that, like those of the Pine Tree Inn, would shortly come to a close.

But for a time, those glory days were glorious indeed.

LIGHTER THAN AIR

Not everyone found the airships that were coming to define Lakehurst welcome. The small village was set on the northern borders of the Pine Barrens, an expansive, desolate, and largely unique forest that dominated central New Jersey. The people of the Pine Barrens – "Pineys," a term of pride when used amongst themselves, and of derision when used by outsiders – were a private people. They wanted little interference from the outside world. They toiled away at their reclusive labors. And sometimes, those labors were illegal.

Moonshining was common in the Pine Barrens. Illegal stills could be found in many a swamp and back road. Police usually turned a blind eye when the locals were involved, but were quick to swoop down on outsiders from up north. So, too, were local quick to mistrust the mighty vessels of the sky.

When the airships of Lakehurst began to coast overhead in the 1930s, Piney moonshiners did not take kindly to what they saw as an intrusion. So they opened fire.

"It was common for the big airships to return to Lakehurst with holes in their envelopes," wrote McPhee. "As the blimps hung over the woods, moonshiners frequently shot at them, in the mistaken belief that the sailors in them were sweeping the woods with binoculars in search of stills."

This unfriendly welcome was uncommon, however. The airships were fast coming to be the image most closely associated with Lakehurst, and why not? The aircraft drew the eye with the slow, graceful bulk. They were a display of power. They instilled a sense of wonder in all who saw them. The airships drew people from near and far. In Lakewood, Boy Scout Dirigible Troop No. 133 existed to help out ground crews and learn about the vessels. A train spur brought sightseers onto the base to see operations there. Kings and queens and other dignitaries rode in the airships. Acclaimed director Frank Capra (*It's A Wonderful Life*, *Mr. Smith Goes To Washington*) even came to Navy Lakehurst to get footage for his 1931 film, *Dirigible*, starring legendary beauty Fay Wray of *King Kong* fame.

For military men and airship aficionados, the airships themselves were just as famous as any king, queen or director. One such historic vessel was the U.S.S. Los Angeles, an American zeppelin that enjoyed the longest career of any rigid airship.

Rigid airships are those with an internal framework over which the outer material is laid. Giant cells, or bags, of gas inside keep the vessel afloat. The few airships seen these days – as of 2007, only about 20 operate worldwide – are essentially inflated bags commonly called "blimps."

The Los Angeles was no blimp. This was a state-of-the-art airship in every way, and the largest aircraft in the world when it first took flight. Though an American vessel, it was not built by Americans. The Germans, originators of the zeppelin design, built the 2,470,000-cubic-foot craft, which was given to the United States as war debt compensation following World War I. The massive ship arrived at Lakehurst in October 1924 after becoming just the fourth aircraft in history to cross the Atlantic Ocean. Once in town, the vessel flew thousands of nautical miles over the course of more than 300 flights, utilizing its crew of about 45 for training and experimental missions. Those missions helped develop military technology that furthered the role of aircraft in combat, building blocks that lead to the great strategic changes spawned by World War II – namely, the vital role air dominance now plays in securing wartime victory. Among the advancements, the U.S.S. Los Angeles was key in the development of improved mooring systems and airplane hook-ups. Biplanes could actually launch from, and hook back up to, the underside of the airship. Airplane pilots would fly underneath the vessels and hook up to a "trapeze" device, which could then pull the fighters into the belly of the craft. For a brief time, airships were the first aircraft carriers, with some airships capable of storing a number of fighters within their framework.

While the Los Angeles was a groundbreaking and historically significant craft, it may be best known for one of the most startling photographs in airship history.

One fiercely windy day, while attached to a tall mooring tower, a gust lifted the giant craft high into the air. The craft's nose, however, was still attached to the mast. Up soared the Los Angeles, up, up, up, until it stood nearly vertical, nose to the mooring tower

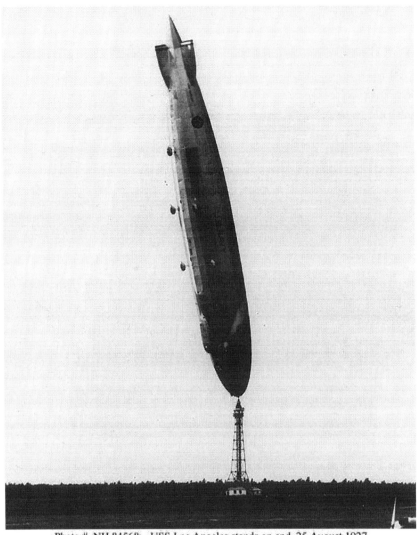

Photo # NH 84568   USS Los Angeles stands on end, 25 August 1927
Photo courtesy of U.S. Naval Historical Center

and tail pointing straight up. It was kept from tumbling off into the nearby pine forest only by the strength of the mast. For several tense minutes it stood on its nose, the crew inside bracing for the worst. An intrepid photographer snapped a now famous picture of the incident, showing the huge airship balancing precariously on a tiny steel tower.

The Los Angeles survived the mishap but would not fly much longer. The craft was decommissioned in 1932, and was disassembled seven years later in Hangar No. 1 after enjoying the longest career of any rigid airship.

Other airships were not so lucky.

Another airship for the history books was the U.S.S. Akron, a scouting vessel constructed by the Goodyear-Zeppelin Corporation in 1931. In October of that year, the 785-foot aircraft flew from its birthplace in Ohio to Lakehurst, where it was stationed next to the U.S.S. Los Angeles. A mast tugged along by a locomotive pulled the vessel into and out of Hangar No. 1.

The Akron arrived at Lakehurst when airship activity was

Photo # NH 42169   Airships Akron and Los Angeles fly over Philadelphia
Photo courtesy of U.S. Naval Historical Center

making its greatest strides. It was to act as a naval scout, scouring the seas for enemy vessels.

At least, that was the intent.

While the Akron's public relations role was a great success, gathering onlookers and receiving rave reviews from journalists, its success as a scouting vessel was questionable at best. Demonstrations for Navy officials in North Carolina and California proved unimpressive. In North Carolina, the Akron was unable to reliably locate "enemy" vessels. In California, drills showed the craft to be extremely vulnerable to attack by airplanes. In a freak mishap, three members of the ground crew were hauled into the sky; two fell to their death. But the tests were not a *total* failure. Charles Rosendahl, commander of the Akron, was among the first to see the wartime potential of such a craft – though few others initially shared his ideas.

The key to what Rosendahl saw that others did not was in how airships used the airplanes they sometimes took with them. Though initially regarded to some degree as failures, the North Carolina and California tests proved Rosendahl's ideas were on target. While other military officials thought the airships should simply transport planes, which would then be launched for scouting missions, Rosendahl thought just the opposite. He said the *airships* should be the craft doing the scouting, while the planes would be there primarily to defend the airship. His vision prevailed, and airships' role in combat was secured.

While it helped pioneer an important though short-lived period in military history, the Akron's military career ended in disaster. In an accident off the Jersey Shore, the airship suffered a combination of harsh weather conditions and control failures that left all but three of its crew dead. It claimed more lives than the famous Hindenburg disaster.

On April 3, 1933, the Akron left Lakehurst for a routine training flight. On board was Admiral William A. Moffett, something of a publicity hound and a huge supporter of Naval airships. So was the popular Lt. Cmdr. Herbert V. Wiley, another strong supporter of lighter-than-air operations.

It was to be a routine flight. There were no indications of hazardous weather conditions. Just off the Atlantic Ocean, however, the airship ran into a severe cold front. Around midnight, the ship's new commanding officer, Frank C. McCord, who had taken over the Akron in January, turned the ship east to rise out the conditions over the sea.

That's when the turbulence hit.

Severe downdrafts pulled the craft towards the ocean. The crew dropped ballast and struggled for control. After dropping to 700 feet, precariously close to the cold ocean waters, the Akron again rose to its 1,600-foot cruising altitude. Or so they thought. In fact, the ship's barometric altimeter was reading hundreds of feet higher than the actual cruising altitude of the craft. The crew tried to fly on, thinking they had risen above trouble, but failed. There was no response from the wheel. Unbeknownst to the crew, the airship's tail had already dipped in the sea.

Moments later, the control car beneath the Akron crashed in to the frigid Atlantic.

The U.S.S. Akron did not carry life jackets. It had just one raft. The April waters were still icy cold.

Seventy-three died when the Akron plunged into the ocean. Some drowned without ever getting out. Others who did escape could not survive the icy ocean waters. Admiral Moffet and C.O. McCord were among those who went down with their ship.

Photo # NH 72639   Naval Reserve O2C-1 aircraft return to base after searching for USS Akron, April 1933
Photo courtesy of U.S. Naval Historical Center

Only three men survived. Among them was Wiley. He would live to fly another day.

And some 24 hours later, the Atlantic Ocean was not quite finished claiming victims. The next day, the U.S. Navy J-3, an open-gondola airship capable of touching down on the water, was involved in the search for survivors. It, too, went down, and both members of its crew perished.

"The loss of the *Akron* with its crew of gallant officers and men is a national disaster," said President Franklin Delano Roosevelt. "I grieve with the Nation and especially with the wives and families of the men who were lost. Ships can be replaced, but the Nation can ill afford to lose such men as Rear Admiral William A. Moffett and his shipmates who died with him upholding to the end the finest traditions of the United States Navy."

In a horrifying coda to the Akron crash, its sister ship, the U.S.S. Macon, crashed into the Pacific in February 1935. Wiley, one of just three survivors of the Akron crash, was once again on board. This accident was less serious, however, and he once again pulled through. Of the Macon's crew of 83, just two crew members perished.

But it was two too many.

With the death of 75 military men off the coast of New Jersey, the worst of a series of accidents, the last days of the Navy's lighter-than-air operations had begun. So, too, did the last days of Lakehurst's heyday as the "airship capital of the world." Few knew it at the time, but the Akron disaster would serve as a precursor to another ill-fated flight that would prove less costly in lives, yet would be far more costly to the public perception of lighter-than-air vessels.

And even as the airships over Lakehurst were enjoying their glorious golden years, the luxurious Pine Tree Inn was also enjoying the last years of its fabulous life.

It, too, would soon disappear from the Lakehurst landscape.

LAST DAYS OF THE PINE TREE INN

In the 1920s and 1930s, as airships sailed quietly overhead, life in Lakehurst was moving forward peacefully. The Naval base was establishing itself as the key provider of jobs in and around town, but the luxurious Pine Tree Inn remained a focal point for borough residents, too.

"In its day, the Inn dominated the downtown area both visually and economically and was a highly unorthodox enterprise in its particular locale," wrote Annette Barbaccia, Executive Director of the NJ Pinelands Commission, in 2001. "A *grande dame* of a building, it catered to the kind of comfortable clientele normally associated with Atlantic City, Miami Beach, and other well-heeled shore towns of that time."

But Lakehurst's days as a resort town were not destined to last. The days of the Pine Tree Inn were numbered. As they waned, the Naval base would more and more become the remaining face of Lakehurst.

For a time, though, the town's famous Navy base and historic inn crossed paths, bringing together two important elements of Lakehurst history. Marshall Sewell, who sometimes played piano at the Inn, recalls that base personnel enjoyed the nightlife the Pine Tree provided. Sailors stationed at the base were routinely seen at the inn's dance hall, which served as a natural center for local

The library of the Pine Treen Inn
Photo courtesy of the Lakehurst Historical Society

Pine Tree Inn, Lakehurst, N. J.

Postcard courtesy of Lakehurst Historical Society

entertainment. The sailors didn't live up to the stereotype of wild and crazy military men, Sewell said, but that didn't stop band members from joking about them.

"Members of Lou Pulcrano's band from Lakewood would joke that they were glad to have an upright piano instead of a baby grand at the Pine Tree Inn. In case the sailors ever started throwing beer bottles, the musicians could take shelter behind the piano," Sewell remembered. "This never happened because the management kept everything in order."

Since the 1890s, the Pine Tree Inn had provided the wealthy with a quiet place to relax, locals with jobs, and Lakehurst itself with a magnificent place to point to with pride.

But times change. The once steady stream of wealthy vacationers fell to a trickle. Finally, in 1934, the Inn ceased operations as a resort.

No more walks for the wealthy along Lake Horicon. No more dance hall. No more Victorian luxury.

It did not disappear straight away, however. The Pine Tree Inn remained a part of Lakehurst for several years after closing its doors.

From 1934 to 1937, the Pine Tree was used as a sewing factory, where scores of Lakehurst and Lakewood residents worked. Verna Thomas, one of the Lakehurst Historical Society's pioneers, worked there. She said on their lunch break, employees would wander through the vacant hotel rooms, taking in final glimpses of the luxury once enjoyed there. Even that was not to last.

In 1937, the Pine Tree Inn was demolished altogether. In its place now stands Lakehurst Elementary School.

But there is a little-known piece of Pine Tree Inn lore: One piece of the inn still stands to this day, located several blocks away from its original location.

"When the hotel faced demolition, its owners saved a small portion of the central section, part of its grand ballroom," Sewell recalled. "This single room contained a bar and dance floor, and for several years was operated as a dance hall, primarily patronized by

The Pine Tree Inn and its associated tennis courts.
Photo courtesy of the Lakehurst Historical Society

sailors from the Naval Air Station and their dates."

There it sat until the 1940s, when Harold Fucile, then mayor of Lakehurst, bought the last remaining portion of the Pine Tree Inn. The once glorious building was lifted out of the ground, placed on huge greased logs, and rolled to Route 70. He renamed it the Chat-A-Way Inn. There it operated for many years as a place for residents to come together for a good time. Ask many an older area resident about the Chat A Way Inn and you'll be greeted with a smile.

Yet that, too, is gone, though what was once the Chat-A-Way Inn remains. The last remaining portion of the once elegant and prestigious Pine Tree Inn currently stands on Route 70, near the Center Street intersection. Throughout the 1980s and 1990s it switched names numerous times, though its business remained consistent through most of those years. It was a strip club, or "go-go bar," catering to biker gangs and those craving a glimpse of flesh. An ignoble end to a once noble place. The club was finally closed down in the 1990s after a much-publicized ruckus involving an out-of-town motorcycle gang. As of this writing, the fate of the building remains in limbo.

Other unseen pieces of the Inn remain, too. In the early 2000s, during the construction of a new wing at Lakehurst Elementary School, a tunnel was discovered beneath the school. At one time, the tunnel provided worker access between the Pine Tree Inn and one of its secondary cottages across Union Avenue. That cottage is now the home of Stephen Childers, former mayor of Lakehurst. He told this author the end of the tunnel can still be seen in his basement; walled up and inaccessible, but clearly visible.

And so ended the illustrious life of the Pine Tree Inn. For almost 40 years, the Pine Tree Inn was a jewel in the pines, bringing folks far and wide by horse-and-buggy, automobile, and, rather significantly, by train.

They would come no more.

But there is one final twist to the story of the Pine Tree Inn. Like 1921's noteworthy historical quirk – the borough was officially incorporated as a municipality the same year the Navy base was officially commissioned – the demolition of the Pine Tree Inn coincides with one of the most significant dates in Lakehurst history. That same year, for the tenth and final time an airship by the name of "Hindenburg" flew into town.

This time, it lit up the Lakehurst skies.

THE TITANIC
OF THE SKIES

The Hindenburg. There is no other person, place, or thing more closely associated with Lakehurst than the massive German airship that tragically became the Titanic of the air.

To this day, it remains the largest vessel ever to take to the skies. It was over 800 feet long; as long as two football fields and the majority of a third. Despite its stunning bulk, it routinely made the flight from Germany to Lakehurst in a mere two days while carrying scores of passengers.

But most notably, it exploded into a ball of flame over Lakehurst on May 6, 1937.

There is no better-known airship in the world. Few disasters have reached its level of recognition. It has even become something of a pop culture icon; an image of the Hindenburg disaster graces the cover of rock and roll legend Led Zeppelin's "Led Zeppelin I" album, hit shows like The Simpsons have parodied the crash, and the famed photograph of the airship in flames has been seen by millions. It is one of the Twentieth Century's most iconic moments.

The Hindenburg was a Nazi vessel, constructed by the Germans in 1935 as the crowning jewel of its vast fleet of zeppelins. It took its name from Paul von Hindenburg, the most famous German general of the First World War, whose name was also given to the Hindenburg Line, or Siegfried Line, of the same war. From the very start the vessel was destined to make history. A contract between the United States Navy and German companies was signed the year of the craft's construction, paving the way for the craft's first trans-Atlantic flight.

And so it came, a beautiful, doomed piece of technology. The initial flight took about 61 hours. The Hindenburg made its first appearance over the Borough of Lakehurst in May 1936, carrying over 100 passengers and crewmen and over 2,000 pounds

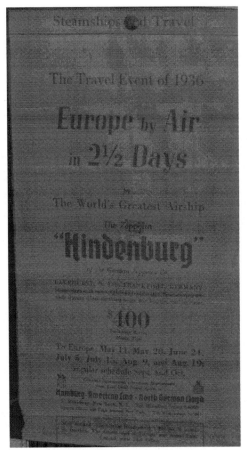

of mail. To help land the massive craft, the German Zeppelin Transport Company hired men from the borough to assist the ground crew. They were paid $1 an hour for their efforts. It was worth it. They had a chance to be part of a historic event. During that first visit, an estimated 75,000 people clamored to the base over the course of three days to see the famous vessel. Dignitaries from all over the nation were on hand to welcome it. After all, Lakehurst was a bona fide international airport, one of the only ones in the Western Hemisphere, and it was welcoming a vessel of distinction.

The Hindenburg was undeniably luxurious for its time. It featured a lounge and dining rooms, a smoking room (right next to thousands of cubic feet of highly flammable hydrogen) and a spectacular viewing room. Chefs prepared gourmet meals. Music played. It was, by all accounts, an elegant affair enjoyed by the rich and privileged. A parallel, some would argue, with the famous Titanic, another absurdly large and luxurious vessel claimed in an unexpected disaster. A round-trip ticket from Germany to America and back again on board the Hindenburg cost $720. Accounting for inflation, that's over $10,000 in 2006 dollars! A big price for a big ship.

Maybe not quite as big as local legend claims, however. Contrary to popular belief, the huge aircraft did in fact fit into the confines of Hangar One. *Barely.* According to the Navy Lakehurst Historical Society, about 15 inches remained between the doors of the hangar and the ends of the craft. It was a tight squeeze, but it fit.

While the story of the Hindenburg disaster has been well told, the vessel did not simply fly into town one day and explode into flame. By the time of the explosion, it had already become inextricably tied with Lakehurst. During 1936 and 1937, the massive aircraft made no less than 10 trips to the small Pine Barrens borough. Over 1,000 passengers made the journey, and mail and freight, including full-sized automobiles, came with them. And those trips drew attention. In the days before television and 24-hour news, a visit by the Hindenburg captured the attention of the entire town. For the people of Lakehurst, a visit by the iconic German vessel was always a treat.

Like so many Lakehurst residents during the 1930s, memories of the Hindenburg remain fresh to Leo Whalen, probably better known to longtime residents as Pete Whalen. Whalen moved out of town in 1941 or so, when he was about 14, but his memories of the Hindenburg and its crew are still vivid. According to Whalen, people would congregate in the streets of town, their eyes turned skyward to watch it pass overhead.

"When that came over, everybody looked. I remember I saw it in the summer of 1936," Whalen said. "I remember the

The Hindenburg and RD-4 shown over Hangar No. 1 in Lakehurst.
Photo courtesy of U.S. Coast Guard

German sailors coming over to my father's store to buy soda and candy and souvenirs to bring back to Germany. I remember them being real sharp in their uniforms."

Wearing polished, pristine uniforms and displaying a by-the-book demeanor, the sailors drew a lot of attention. They were nice young men, Whalen remembered; the notion of what a Nazi was had not yet swept across the world. By 1939, people would no longer think of them the same way, but for now they were sharp sailors of the sky flying in from across the sea. They must have seemed almost alien to the natives of the small pines community. Aliens visiting from a vessel the likes of which none had ever before seen.

The Hindenburg's dominance of the skies would not last very long.

On May 3, 1937, the German craft took off from its airfield in Frankfurt and made a seemingly routine voyage across the Atlantic. Nothing unusual about that. It was the tenth time it had made the journey. About twenty or so trans-Atlantic trips were planned for the year, seventeen of them scheduled to go to Lakehurst, the others to South America. This was nothing more than a just another voyage.

Three days later, the disaster about which volumes have been written occurred.

Nicolas Rakoncza, a retired Navy airman, was just five years old when the Hindenburg flew into Lakehurst on that fateful day. He was in Woodbridge, New Jersey, at the time, watching as the craft came in from the direction of Staten Island.

"One thing I remember was the sound of the engines. I had never heard anything like them. It wasn't a whine. These were *diesel* engines," Rakoncza said. "I remember the windows were open. You could see the passengers waving their handkerchiefs to the people below."

The memory stuck with Rakoncza, yet none were as touched by the disaster as those who saw it unfold before their very eyes.

John Iannaccone was one of those people. Iannaccone began his career at Navy Lakehurst in 1929 and, as of this writing, still assists the base to this day. He knew his airships; he served on the U.S.S. Los Angeles, bouncing back and forth between Lakehurst and the west coast. He *still* knows airships; few local authorities are better respected. And he knows the Hindenburg disaster. In May 1937, he had a better view of the Hindenburg than most, serving on the mooring mast crew tasked with helping land the ship.

Also on the ground were Herbert Morrison and his sound engineer, Charlie Nehlson, both from a Chicago radio station. They were in Lakehurst to witness the majestic Hindenburg arrive. Watching the events of the day unfold, Morrison ended up making one of the most recognizable news broadcasts of the last 100 years, his words "oh, the humanity" becoming a cultural landmark.

Verna Thomas also watched from the field at Hangar No. 1, a witness to the terrific spectacle that was to come.

And a short mile or so away, watching from the quiet confines of the Borough of Lakehurst, were scores of town residents, gathered in the streets and on roofs and just outside their favorite watering hole. Among them was Whalen. That massive, majestic vessel was once against coasting triumphantly into town. And then something happened.

"I was looking at it with my cousin with binoculars," Whalen recalled. "And then we could see the explosion, the fire."

The Hindenburg, the largest aircraft ever to take flight, was on fire.

Flame and disaster began to rain from the sky.

This is Lakehurst's signature moment. The moment most intertwined with the town. It came on May 6, 1937. On that day, the Hindenburg, an 800-foot German zeppelin, exploded into a ball of flame.

It was overcast when the craft sailed in, raining intermittently, but the weather was manageable and improving. At this point, the trip was probably routine for crew members both in the craft and on the ground, so the weather wasn't a great concern. The vessel carried 97 people on board.

Below, a throng of spectators were gathered on the field behind Hangar No. 1. On the ground watching along with the others were broadcaster Morrison and Nehlson, covering the event for their Chicago radio station. The work they did that day has become legendary. As Morrison watched the Hindenburg cruise into town, all seemed well.

"What a great sight it is, a thrilling one, just a marvelous sight," Morrison broadcast. "It's coming down out of the sky, pointed directly towards us and toward the mooring mast. The mighty diesel motors just roared, the propellers biting into the air and throwing it back into a gale-like whirlpool. No wonder this great floating palace can travel through the air at such a speed, with these powerful motors behind it."

He described the sun's reflection off the observation deck windows as "sparkling like glittering jewels" and the vast field below, where scores of workers were on hand for the ship's mooring, as "a moving mass of cooperative action." What a sight it must have been.

Even as the broadcast went on, John Iannaccone was part of the mass of cooperation Morrison described, working with the mooring mast crew to help haul in the airship. By 1937, Iannaccone had already worked with airships for nearly a decade, among them the magnificent U.S.S. Los Angeles. He had hauled in aircraft and battled winds and knew how airships behaved. He wasn't seeing anything he hadn't seen before. But that would soon change.

Meanwhile, Morrison was painting a vivid picture for his listeners. The Hindenburg was "riding majestically toward us like some great feather, riding as though it was mighty good, mighty proud of the place it's playing in the world's aviation." He talked about the important personnel on board and described the mooring ropes dropping from the nose of the ship, the very same mooring ropes with which Iannaccone was working. For a brief moment he mentioned the start of rain – and then in mid thought the broadcast changed.

"It's starting to rain again; the rain had slacked up a little bit. The back motors of the ship are just holding it, just enough to keep it from —

"It burst into flames! Get out of the way! Get out of the way!" Morrison wailed. "Get this, Charlie! Get this, Charlie! It's on fire and it's crashing! It's crashing terrible! Oh, my! Get out of the way, please! It's burning, bursting into flames and is falling on the mooring mast, and all the folks agree that this is terrible. This is the worst of the worst catastrophes in the world! Oh, it's crashing ... oh, four or five hundred feet into the sky, and it's a terrific crash, ladies and gentlemen. There's smoke, and there's flames now, and the frame is crashing to the ground, not quite to the mooring mast ... Oh, the humanity, and all the passengers screaming around here!"

Morrison, a longtime broadcaster and a true professional, was completely caught up in the moment, giving his emotional response to the disaster as it happened. Many of his panicked comments were directed towards Charlie Nehlson, his sound engineer. Audio historian Michael Biel of Morehead State University credits Nehlsen with playing a vital role in ensuring that the key moments of the event were recorded. Because of the era's primitive technology, failing to get the recording would have been very easy. Disturb the equipment just a little, and the moment in history is lost. Despite the death and fire before him, Nehlsen was up to the task.

Morrison, meanwhile, had dropped the cool demeanor of the broadcast journalist. For a man paid to speak, the scene became almost too horrific for words.

"It's -- I can't talk, ladies and gentlemen. Honest, it's just laying there, a mass of smoking wreckage, and everybody can hardly breathe and talk ... I, I'm sorry," Morrison broadcast. "Honest, I can hardly breathe. I'm going to step inside where I cannot see it. Charlie, that's terrible. I -- Listen folks, I'm going to have to stop for a minute, because I've lost my voice. This is the worst thing I've ever witnessed."

Down, down rained the fire and debris and wreckage. Down came the bodies. Down came death. As it fell, the smoldering remains of the massive craft were raining down upon the dozens below. Burning cinders and framework, and even *people*, trying in futility to leap to safety.

But even as the airship fell, Iannaccone did not turn and run. He sprang into action.

"As most people at the scene were running from underneath the enormous airship as it began its fiery 30-second decent into history, Iannaccone observed what was happening from the mooring mast and began rescuing survivors," Thomas Worsdale, former Public Affairs Officer at the Navy base, wrote in 2002 about Iannaccone's efforts.

People had to be pulled away; jumpers rescued. The smoke was terrific. The fumes stifling. It must have seemed a hell on

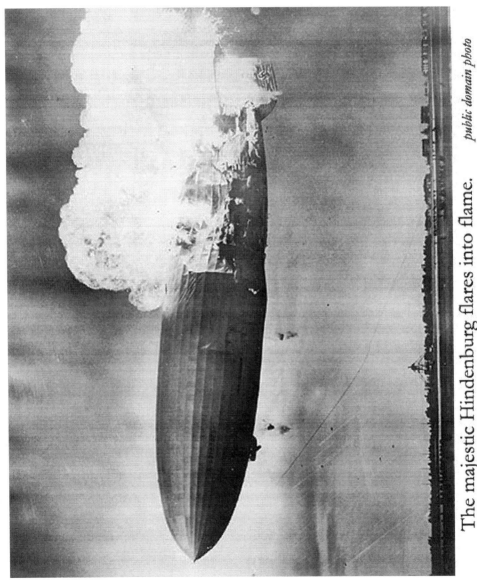

The majestic Hindenburg flares into flame.   *public domain photo*

Earth. Iannaccone was in the middle of it, helping pull survivors away from the wreckage.

And then it was finished. As big as the event looms in aviation history, it was over in a matter of moments. Flamed out, and died.

Herbert Morrison and Charlie Nehlson, broadcasting on site after the disaster.
Photo courtesy of U.S. Naval Institute and the Naval History & Heritage Command

"By the time it hit the ground, it was out," Iannaccone said. "It burned that quick."

In just 37 seconds, the Hindenburg was lost.

With it went 36 victims.

What ensued in the wake of the disaster was plenty of talk, lots of panic, and theories that persist to this very day, but very few answers.

At the time, sabotage was the suspected cause of the disaster. Longtime Lakehurst resident Verna Thomas remembered the entire site being sealed off for days while German officials scrambled to get to Lakehurst and conduct an investigation. With Nazi Germany on the cusp of beginning its attempted conquest of Europe, paranoia was high. There was plenty of suspicion – some even named names – but little in the way of solid evidence to support the sabotage theory. The theory still surfaces from time to time, tickling the fancy of those who like a sinister edge to their disasters, but most serious scholars have long since dismissed the idea.

If it wasn't sabotage, many thought the cause of the blaze that consumed the German zeppelin was the highly flammable hydrogen used to keep the vessel aloft. It was certainly a reasonable conclusion. Rather than the less volatile helium used by the U.S. Navy, the Hindenburg used hydrogen. The Germans were forced to, in fact, because with Hitler in power the United States would not sell helium to Germany. Some have theorized that static electricity in the air that day generated by the overcast conditions ignited leaking hydrogen, setting the whole craft ablaze.

Over 60 years later, however, a new and increasingly accepted theory has all but set aside previous notions about the cause of the Hindenburg disaster.

The cause of the disaster, some theorize, lies not within the massive craft, but without. The outer material of the Hindenburg was a fabric draped over the ship's steel infrastructure. The fabric painted with a cellulose nitrate doping compound and powdered aluminum.

It turns out the compound was also highly flammable.

So flammable, in fact, that preserved fabric samples have been found to still be volatile even 60 years later. In studies conducted on those samples, when the highly-charged atmospheric conditions present during the Hindenburg's explosion were

Photo # NH 57961 Official investigation board for the airship Hindenburg disaster, 27 May 1937
Photo courtesy of U.S. Naval Historical Center

replicated in a lab, the samples burned up within seconds. The Hindenburg, it seems, may have exploded into a ball of flame due to a combination of the highly flammable doping compound and static electricity in the air. Mother Nature met man-made ingenuity. Disaster was the result.

Even with that theory offering what may be the most logical explanation for the disaster, people continue to debate what caused the Hindenburg's explosion. We will probably never truly know its cause. What we do know is the ramifications of the calamity. Highlighted by dramatic photos and a gut-wrenching broadcast, the accident was impossible to ignore. The world saw the virtual death of the airship in its aftermath.

The Hindenburg's legacy has lived on not only through its impact on the course of aviation, but also in broadcasting, image, and the way news now unfolds before our very eyes. Morrison's radio recording, for instance, while becoming famous for its emotion and impact, also serves as a landmark in broadcasting history. It was the first news event recorded live for later radio broadcast. According to the Library of Congress, the broadcast "was the first exception to network radio's ban on the airing of recordings." That is exactly how most radio news is now handled. Morrison – and with him, *Lakehurst* – was first.

Meanwhile, Iannaccone, like many Hindenburg disaster witnesses, has spent a lifetime telling his story. Since retiring, first as a Chief Petty Officer then as a civil servant, he has spent more than 30 years as an expert in lighter-than-air operations, offering firsthand accounts to historians about the airships that have made Lakehurst famous. Iannaccone has offered his vivid memory to television productions for the History, Discovery and Learning channels, as well as C-SPAN and CNN. Programs like *National Geographic*, *Modern Marvels* and *Great Disasters* have featured his recollections. He even had a road named after him. One of the entrances to Navy Lakehurst is called Iannaccone Way in honor of the some 70 years Iannaccone gave to operations there. And to this very day, he volunteers for the Lakehurst Historical Society at its museum in the Borough of Lakehurst, sharing his memories and gladly answering questions for visitors.

At the Lakehurst Historical Society museum, Center Street, visitors can see pieces of wreckage from the Hindenburg, view guest books from the legendary vessel, and see the last remnants of its luxury in pieces of silverware and other items.

Following the disaster, the allure of the airship started to wane. The Akron may have been a bigger tragedy in terms of lives lost, but the Hindenburg happened in front of a huge audience, and thanks to Morrison's recording reached an even larger audience who would never forget the stark images from that day. The world saw lighter than air vessels fail in the most spectacular of ways. People must have been shocked. Certainly it was a blow to the Navy's already troubled airship operations. Though they would linger on for many years, the famous disaster was the signal that the military's exploration of airship potential had come to an end.

Still, the world's fascination with airships did not end. People remain fascinated with blimps, zeppelins, and yes, with the Hindenburg. The vessel and its tragic end have resulted in a slew of books, magazine articles, and even motion pictures. The Hindenburg's legacy endures – and maybe largest of all for a small town called Lakehurst.

Yet for the millions of words written about the Hindenburg disaster, it is but one single moment in the borough's history. Arguably the single most defining moment, yes, but still merely a single moment in what is a rich and interesting history.

The Hindenburg died. But the people of Lakehurst lived on. Life in their small town would continue to change.

THE GHOSTS OF HANGAR NO. 1

Hell rained from the sky. A cavern of flame opened, arms of twisting steel reaching out from within, and from the blazing fireball fell bodies. Fell, or leaped, fleeing the flame and embracing the cold, hard ground hundreds of feet below.

On May 6, 1937, the Hindenburg, crowning jewel of the Nazi rigid airship fleet, exploded in flame over the small town of Lakehurst, New Jersey. In just thirty-seven seconds, the Titanic of the skies was destroyed, taking thirty-six lives with it.

Not all of those thirty-six perished in the initial inferno. As those who were there remember, many of the burned and mangled victims clung to life even as the wreckage smoldered. They were taken to a temporary medical center set up in nearby Hangar No. 1. As the day progressed, the hangar became a morgue. It was an ugly duty for a proud structure. At the time of its construction in 1921, Hangar No. 1 was the largest manmade indoor space in the world and the only hangar in North America capable of housing the massive Hindenburg. It is now on the National Register of Historic Places.

It is also haunted.

None can say who or what haunts the desolate old hangar, though the stories have dogged it for years. That should come as no surprise. Though it is still the largest structure on an active military base, the sprawling interior of Hangar No. 1 is all but empty. Voices die in the heavy air within. Sunlight barely penetrates its lonely haze. Near two hundred feet above, crumbling catwalks glare brokenly at the cobblestone floor below. A cold mist clings to that floor, groping at ankles like a restless memory. To hear that restless spirits dwell in this place is far from shocking.

One lonely evening something in the mists gave a man warmth. A maintenance man (who did not wish for his name to be used) was working the corridors lining the sides of the hangar. He had forgotten something in the hangar. A tool, maybe. A coffee cup. Whatever it was no longer matters. All that matters is that this forgotten object lured him back into the darkened hangar. He ventured in without a jacket, the bitter cold raising goose pimples across his arms. And then he felt a hand upon his shoulder. He felt its warmth coursing through him. He turned. Looked.

No one was there.

Whatever he had forgotten could wait. He wasn't staying there, in that place where the air was dead and cold and charred bodies once exhaled their last breaths. He left. Quickly. As he passed the threshold of the door between the hangar and the connecting offices, the warmth caressing his shoulder disappeared. He was again cold. Cold, and alone. "I don't know what's out there," he said, "and I don't want to know."

He wasn't alone in his experience. As Navy veteran Don Adams recalls, Hangar No. 1 briefly served as a morgue, the results of a disaster that still cannot be explained. Do the ghosts of Hangar No. 1 originate from the now unassuming rooms once used to house those who fell like angels in flame? Some believe they do. Maybe a clue lies with the ghosts.

A long passage once spanned the length of the over eight hundred-foot-long hangar. To this day the doors of what's left of the passage are still prone to sudden and violent slamming as if restless and angry. A Navy man once walked along this passage in the late evening, at first alone. Then in the distance he saw a fellow Navy man walking towards him. The stranger was in archaic dress blues. A set of half-wings was pinned to the uniform, signifying a certified balloon pilot.

But the last Navy blimp was decommissioned in 1962. There were no more Navy balloon pilots.

The man in the old dress blues approached. He was offered a "hello." No response. Kept walking. And passed through the startled onlooker, who turned and saw that the balloon pilot was gone.

Retired airman Nicolas Rakoncza, who at five saw the Hindenburg fly overhead on the day of the disaster, says such stories go back decades. If there is anything to explain the stories, he says the doomed airship fits. Not only were bodies from the disaster brought inside the hangar, not only did some die within, but the disaster itself happened just outside its doors. A memorial rests in the swaying grass outside, within sight of the Hangar No. 1 floor, a small, unassuming memorial to those who perished in a violent hell on Earth.

Yet if the ghosts of Hangar No. 1 truly can be explained by the Hindenburg disaster -- the most famous disaster at Navy Lakehurst, but not the worst connected to the rigid airships that once flew there; that dubious honor goes to the U.S.S. Akron and its seventy-three victims -- why would they enjoy an evening of music and revelry? That's the story told by a Navy veteran who had a late night encounter with a party that wasn't.

A new training facility had opened in offices on the far side of the hangar. Working late one evening, he heard music and voices in the distance. Thinking it a celebration to welcome the new class, he decided to stop in. He could hear the party from behind an office door. He opened it -- and all went silent. The music stopped. The voices stopped.

He was alone in Hangar No. 1.

Or rather, he was alone <u>with</u> Hangar No. 1.

LAST DAYS OF THE RAILROAD

The Pine Tree Inn may have closed shop and the Hindenburg disaster may have signaled the end of the Golden Age of the Airship, but for the people of Lakehurst, time marched on.

Lakehurst has long been associated with lighter-than-air ships. Were it not airships that became the symbol of Lakehurst, however, it may have been the locomotive. Airships made for a unique symbol for the borough, but even in the post-Torrey years, trains were its lifeblood. The railroad was arguably the most vital part of the borough's economy, providing jobs for many residents and customers for business.

That is, of course, something Lakehurst has in common with many small 19th Century American towns. Railroads were an integral part of the American economy in the 1800s, and were a key part of the remarkable growth the nation saw during those 100 years of expansion. Rails tied together faraway places and provided for the birth of the modern economy. Goods could be transported faster. Industry could locate in more remote locations. Population centers no longer needed to be tied together in clusters. Trains became the thread with which the Industrial Revolution was sewn, affording new industries the ability to succeed in ways impossible before America was spider webbed with rail lines.

The nationwide trend held true on the local level. The railroad played an important part in the borough throughout the decades both before and after the turn-of-the-century, through the Great Depression, right up to the post-War years. Isolated in Pine Barrens in the days before superhighways and automobiles, the railroad was the primary means of shipping and transportation throughout central New Jersey.

Lakehurst's prime years as a center of railroading may have fallen by the wayside in the 1860s when the dreams of William

Torrey faltered and faded, but according to longtime area resident Verna Thomas, right into the 1920s, 30s, and 40s, trains remained key to keeping Lakehurst a bustling community.

"In the early 20s, we were the buying center because of the railroad," Thomas said.

For decades, residents made their living through the rails in one way or another. Merchants survived in part through the business the rails brought them. People in town had jobs working on, for, or in support of the railroad. Without the railroad, the borough would have been a far different place. While the only obvious links to Lakehurst's railroad-based past are on Union and Brown avenues, where tracks still function, albeit infrequently, at one time the borough's relationship with trains was impossible to ignore.

The town's railroad facilities were extensive for a town so small. A turntable and roundhouse, shops and maintenance facilities, and more were on hand to keep trains up and running. The train station and roundhouse was located off Fays Lane, the small, barely paved street that runs parallel to Union Avenue on the south side of town. Up until the 1990s, in fact, portions of the structure's foundations could still be seen and were frequently explored by area youth. This author fondly recalls climbing over piles of old stone and into rotting foundations.

How ingrained were the trains to life in Lakehurst? So much so that kids in town rode the train to school. Before the construction of Manchester Township High School in the 1970s, teenagers in Lakehurst and Manchester attended high school in Lakewood. But for a time, students did not make their way to school by bus. During the 1920s and 30s, it was the railroad that served as students' "school bus," dropping them off several blocks away from Lakewood high school, then located on Princeton Avenue. Busses did not begin operation until the 1940s, when Lincoln Transit began driving children to school. According to old-timer Marshall Sewell, many longtime Lakehurst residents still attend class reunions for their Lakewood alma mater.

And just as Lakehurst can boast visits by "celebrity" airships, for a time the community often welcomed a "celebrity locomotive" that became a symbol of an era long since passed.

From 1929 to 1941, Lakehurst was one of the stopping points of The Blue Comet, a fabulously luxurious locomotive that catered to the upper crust of society. Running regularly between Atlantic City and Lakewood – most of the tracks that comprised that route have long since been lost to Mother Nature and development – the train was a frequent visitor to Lakehurst, bringing the wealthy to relax on the grounds of the Pine Tree Inn, north to the resorts of Lakewood, or south to the boardwalk of Atlantic City. (For a time, the train ventured as far north as Elizabethport and Red Bank.) The three locomotives that shared hauling duty were beauties, and so were its passenger cars. It was painted blue. In fact, everything was decorated in blue, right down

The Blue Comet.   *Photo courtesy of Lakehurst Historical Society*

to the napkins and plates in the luxurious dining cars. "The cars had blue seats and carpets, and even the ticket and porters' uniforms were blue. Each car was named after a known comet," Treese wrote in *Trains of New Jersey*. All that blue was trimmed with cream and lettered in dazzling gold.. The plush seats were lovely.

The Blue Comet oozed class.

The train was the brainchild of R.B. White, then president of the Central Railroad of New Jersey. With dreams of providing an experience like no other, he set out to create a train that would rival the legendary luxury of the Titanic – without the ship's nasty sinking problem.

Not that sinking was an issue. There are, after all, no icebergs on New Jersey's rail lines.

No icebergs, but plenty of rain. On August 19, 1939, a train hauling Comet cars derailed near Chatsworth after heavy rains had washed out the tracks. "Most of the injured passengers had been riding in the observation car and were struck by the loose wicker chairs, which flew in all directions," wrote author Anthony J. Bianculli in his work, *Iron Rails in the Garden State: Tales of New Jersey Railroading*. "The dining car was badly damaged and was withdrawn from service."

According to Barbara Solem-Stull, "There was no loss of life, even though early news reports suggested the casualties were enormous."

Some might say the derailment was an omen. Passenger trains to Lakehurst, upscale or not, were not to last.

Without the railroad, Lakehurst would not be the community it is today. Yet the days when the rails were central to day-to-day life in the small pinelands borough are long since passed, the remnants of the days when locomotives were a routine sight. Among them, the Blue Comet.

Initially, the legendary locomotive was "just passing through." During its first few years, the Blue Comet accepted no passengers for any station on its route save at Atlantic City, much to the disappointment of Lakewood and Lakehurst hotel owners. The train would stop in Lakehurst, but only to take in water at the borough's maintenance facility. The Blue Comet would then speed south through Whitings (as it was then called, named after Nathan C. Whiting, who came to the area in 1852 to work the lumber industry) and Chatsworth at 70 to 80 miles per hour, racing to Atlantic City. Even so, it was an attraction for locals.

"As it raced through the Pine Barrens, trains crews would toss their newspapers to some of the locals who lived in remote areas far from a newsstand," wrote Bianculli. In return, crews might fund buckets of blueberries waiting for them along their route.

It's no wonder the train drew attention. According to Bianculli, 'The company went all out to promote it. The locomotives were fitted with distinctive whistles, and its schedule was posted at highway crossings so that viewers could time their arrival to catch a glimpse of the train as it sped by."

The company took promotions even further, staging a race between the train and an airplane flown by aviatrix Mrs. Keith Miller.

Miller lost.

In 1930, the famed Lionel Trains even produced a model train of the Blue Comet.

None of this would last. With the establishment of air travel to Florida, the train's Atlantic City business started to decline. The economic downturn of the 1930s could not have helped matters. With business slumping, the Central Railroad agreed to stop at Lakewood, Lakehurst, Red Bank and other stations on the Comet's route, picking up "ordinary" passengers.

But soon, no passengers would be picked up at all, ordinary or otherwise.

"Even the classy Blue Comet could not overcome the Depression's effect on vacation passenger business," Treese wrote in *Railroads of New Jersey*. Thanks to that and mounting competition from other lines, "By the late 1930s, the famous Blue Comet was operating at a loss, and in 1939, the CNJ petitioned to abandon the service."

White succeeded only briefly in his dream to operate a luxury passenger train. It was not to last largely due to The Blue Comet's inability to turn a profit. Maybe it is because White's dream was simply too elaborate and too grand. The luxury was so painstakingly thorough and expensive, and the timing so utterly bad – it took its first run in 1929, just nine months before Black Tuesday and the start of the Great Depression – the train only managed to operate until September 1941, when it made its final run.

Like the Pine Tree Inn, the Blue Comet luxury train did not end its days quickly or with the same "elite status" it once enjoyed. In its final years, the classy engine became just another people mover. Verna Thomas recalled that just before the Blue Comet made its last run, Lakehurst kids were riding to school on the luxury steam train. Until the 40s and 50s, when an actual school bus took up the responsibility, the Blue Comet was for some little more than an elaborate school bus.

The Blue Comet faded from history not with a bang, but with a whimper.

When the Blue Comet officially ended its scheduled runs, its unique blue and gold coaches were added to the Central Jersey Railroad's regular runs, hauled by "ordinary" locomotives. Even after World War II, commuters from Ocean County to New York were enjoying the comfortable blue velvet-like seats left over from the Comet.

Its three locomotives were also put into less prestigious service. At least one of the locomotives that powered the Blue Comet, Pacific locomotive No. 831, was still hauling cars in North Jersey many years after the Blue Comet itself was gone. No longer blue and luxurious, an image of it sitting amongst weed-strewn tracks in Elizabethport in 1955 made it "difficult to image the locomotive's glorious past," according to author Charles P. Caldes.

But even without White's Blue Comet, rails long played a strong part in the life of a Lakehurst resident. From jobs to goods to transportation, trains were a daily sight. Yet change is inevitable, and the world was changing. Air travel began. The automobile became commonplace. As transportation technology became accessible to everyday people, what were once vast distances became smaller. And things just kept changing. Economic woes troubled the country, quickly followed by war. In the face of that changing world, the railroad as residents knew it would not last.

By the end of the 1940s, the railroad was dying in Lakehurst. In 1952, passenger service to Lakehurst ceased altogether.

These days, the remnants of the rail era are all but gone, visible only in some infrequently used rail spurs and crumbling ruins hidden from view in dense woods. There is no longer any sign of the train station once situated off Fays Lane, behind the borough parking lot. Even the remains of the foundation, once easily accessible, have been removed. Only one major structure remains. Hidden away in the woods behind the post office, nestled between the two forks of the Union Avenue tracks (one spur continues on to Whiting, while the other curves away to the Toms River area), lies an aging reminder of Lakehurst's historic link with the rail industry. Standing in the midst of overgrown, tick-infested forest are a series of concrete pillars some 10 to 12 feet tall. They rest on a long, tall platform also made of concrete. The pillars and platform seem out of place in the otherwise quiet stretch of woods; no tracks lead to the structure. No roads. No paths. To access it, one must either climb through thorny underbrush at the Whiting spur or climb across a burned, ruined trestle hidden to the right of the Toms River spur. The ruin is now covered in vines, broken glass and spray paint. At one time, however, it was an important part of train operations in the borough. Tracks branched off the main line and led to this platform, which was designed to give trains a place to dump their ashes. Locomotives would pull up, dispose of their ashes in a massive holding bin, and be ready to move on. It's a silent, hidden reminder of what once was.

A few small slices of what was once the Blue Comet's

The roundhouse and related workshops that once lined the rails in downtown Lakehurst. Little to no trace of these structures remain.
Photo courtesy of Lakehurst Historical Society

luxury can still be seen, too, albeit not in Lakehurst itself. In recent years, a Blue Comet observation car has been restored for excursions with the Cape May Seashores Lines. Another car can be seen off Route 78, at the Clinton Station Diner, where an original Blue Comet car juts from the building. The railroad car "survived years of abandonment before getting an extreme makeover from the current owner," according to Treese

Of course, trains never *fully* left the Borough of Lakehurst, though they are seen now only infrequently. The existing lines are no longer used for passenger service. Instead, Conrail utilizes them for freight, keeping in continuous if not regular operation since the heyday of high-class luxury trains. Once in a while, a row of freight cars can still be seen beneath the Route 70 bridge, luring train lovers or Lakehurst's youth. Catch one at just the right time and you just might meet an engineer willing to show you around the cab of the locomotive.

Will passenger trains ever return to Lakehurst? The tracks are still there, after all. The answer is a qualified "maybe." The town's history with passenger trains has reared its head in the present day. Through the late 1990s and into the early part of the new century, a growing movement is acting to once again bring passenger rail service to Lakehurst. Bills have been signed, funding approved, and plans have been outlined for rail service linking Lakehurst to lines operating in the northern part of the state. It's not as far-fetched as it sounds, though it remains a decade away as of this writing. The so-called "MOM" rail line, or Monmouth-Ocean-Middlesex, has hit roadblock after roadblock, but it keeps inching steadily forward. Lawmakers want it. New Jersey Transit, which would operate the line, wants it. The people of the area want it.

So ... maybe, just *maybe*, history may again live.

Of course, the conversation over the MOM rail line is well over a decade old as of this writing and shows little sign of progressing forward. By 2011, talks about returning the line to service had ground to a standstill. Where once it was an issue frequently touched on by those in elected office, most officials don't even bother to bring it up anymore. And why should they? Eleven full years after some officials suggested real progress was right around the corner, the project appears dead.

But that is another story for another time.

Yes, in the early part of the 20th Century there were trains, resorts and airships. Yet there was another side of Lakehurst. While the Pine Tree Inn and the Blue Comet operated in luxury and the Navy began building history in the skies above, residents of the small borough, like people all across America, were worrying about problems much larger than which gorgeous room to stay in and what time to take tea at Lake Horicon. They were coping with the devastating impact of the Great Depression.

DEPRESSION YEARS

In the early years of the 21st Century, Lakehurst has become yet another of Ocean County's so-called "bedroom communities," populated with blue and white collar families commuting out of town to make a living. Home is a place to eat and sleep, and not much else.

Such was not always the case. In the past, residents rarely strayed far for work. Made up of working-class folks and merchants who routinely got their hands dirty for a living, Lakehurst had industry enough to keep a good slice of the populace employed. The railroad, local factories, and the Naval base were all sources of regular work, a sometimes scarce commodity in the Pine Barrens.

For one tough stretch of years, though, *any* source of jobs would have been welcome.

In 1937, the Hindenburg crashed. But just under a decade prior, a different crash had a bigger impact on the daily lives of Lakehurst residents. One bigger than the crash of any zeppelin, no matter how historic, ever could.

On October 24, 1929, the stock market began a rapid decline. Several days of escalating panic built one upon the next. On October 29, a day now called "Black Tuesday," the market collapsed altogether. The day would become the best-known precursor to one of America's most difficult periods. The Great Depression. It was a time that ravaged the nation's economy, put men out of work and families out of home. From 1929 to 1932, the average American's income was nearly cut in half. By 1933, some 25 percent of Americans were unemployed. Work of any kind, no matter how menial, no matter how difficult, was a great gift. John Steinbeck's "The Grapes of Wrath," a chronicle of an Okalahoma family forced off of their farm, is among the most recognizable chronicles of the American experience during the Depression. Lakehurst's experience obviously differs from that presented in Steinbeck's classic, a story of ups, downs, and unique solutions to the era's problems. But that doesn't mean times were not tough.

A postcard-perfect view of downtown
Lakehurst early in the 20th Century.
Photo courtesy of the Lakehurst Historical Society

Tough, but manageable. According to longtime resident Verna
Thomas, life seemed much simpler then, even through the tough
times of the Great Depression.

As elsewhere, life in Lakehurst during the Depression was
not easy. Jobs were scarce. Many homes did not even have
electricity. Most of Lakehurst's residents just made ends meet
through hard work, family, and friends, including the people who
lived in "Chief City," an obscure name for the area of Lakehurst
near Lake Horicon where the "better-off" lived. And surviving
often meant being creative. Thomas tells a story about one tough
winter and the lengths low-income families had to go to in order to
survive.

Hunting was an essential part of life for many citizens of the
Pine Barrens. Those in town who did not rely on government
subsidized meat — canned horsemeat — would eat venison (deer
meat) throughout the cold months between December and

February. (Venison remains common in the Ocean County area, which boasts a large hunting population despite a changing regional demographic.) In the 1920s and 1930s, however, many families were unable to afford an icebox, so other means had to be found to keep the meat through the winter. Lakehurst families would put the venison in burlap sacks, which were tied shut and affixed with a rope. The meat would then be hung into Horicon Stream, which flows behind Union and Brown avenues from Lake Horicon, joining the Union Branch of the Toms River. The creek's frigid waters would keep the meat almost as well as an icebox.

But wouldn't the much needed meat be stolen? Not according to Thomas. In those days, she said, people had more respect for one another's belongings, especially in a community as small and close-knit as Lakehurst. Everybody had their spot along the creek, and that spot always remained undisturbed and untouched.

That kind of neighborly treatment was common in those days, Thomas said, especially during the Depression. It was a time when citizens had to help one another out to make it through lean years.

According to Thomas, local merchants would quietly forgive the debts of families in need. In the days before credit cards, when a resident did not have the money necessary for groceries, the shop owner would record the amount in a ledger. A small town courtesy in a place where everyone knew everyone else. Usually, such debts were paid quickly. During the Depression, however, some families *never* had enough money to feed and cloth themselves. Yet people looked out for one another. Those with means helped in small, quiet ways. Many of Lakehurst's merchants would simply wipe away that debt as if it had never existed, helping neighbors struggling to make it through another month.

Even following the Depression years, Lakehurst remained a tight, close community.

In 2000, the late Gladys Prosperi, a longtime resident of the area, told this author that the feeling in Lakehurst and other small towns was that of an extended family. Everyone knew one another's name. Everyone was available for a neighbor.

"It was like a family, almost," Prosperi said. "There isn't enough of that these days."

Of course, in those days, a family-like atmosphere almost couldn't be helped. One phone line served an entire block of houses, allowing neighbors to listen in on one another's conversations. With most everyone both living in and working in town, it was near impossible to not know something about just about all of your neighbors. Community was the order of the day. Even when extra spending money was all but nonexistent, people in town found a way to remain close. Social gatherings and civic events were a time to catch up with people you hadn't spoken to in a while. For a time, one of the many lodges in the borough was a prime center for entertainment and community spirit. The Red Men's Lodge hall, now the Fleet Reserve building on Union Avenue, used to host many such social gatherings. Even for folks who lived just outside of Lakehurst, the hall was someplace to have a good time.

"When I was a young girl, I used to go there and dance with the boys. It was always fun," Prosperi said. "It's a beautiful building ... It's like home."

In supporting one another, she said, the people of Lakehurst kept spirits high during a period when American spirits had ebbed to a terrible low. Helping out neighbors. Sharing in the love of a community. Making the best with what limited resources you had.

That was Lakehurst during the Depression.

THINGS TO
MAKE AND DO

From the late 1920s and into the 1930s, Great Eastern Airways operated the "Lakehurst Airport" on Route 571, between Route 547 and Alligator Road. For a mere $3, Great Eastern would fly passengers over the area, offering a bird's eye view of Lakehurst.

What would greet the eye from well above the borough below? On the surface, not much at all. Mostly trees and trains, separated by clusters of modest homes. But bubbling beneath the veil of pine trees and train tracks would have been a series of small, personal, interconnected stories. The very heart of Lakehurst. Indeed, more than trains and blimps and trees, the beating heart of Lakehurst was in the people that populated the close-knit community.

Leo Whalen is a Lakehurst boy who made a name for himself. "Lucky Leo," to be precise. Yes, the Lucky Leo of Seaside Heights boardwalk fame, a name recognizable to any who have enjoyed some time on the Jersey Shore's popular Seaside Heights boardwalk.

But longtime Lakehurst residents would better know him as Pete Whalen. Once a Hibernia Avenue resident, years ago his father owned a shop called — you guessed it — Whalen's, and in 1932 built the place that would eventually become Weaver's, a once-popular downtown pub now since replaced with townhouses. There, as they would for decades, Lakehurst residents enjoyed good times together. The small tavern featured a dance floor, a bar and tables where people could eat. Locals mingled with personnel from the Navy base, including a young Whalen, who was already off to a good start in the world of gaming.

"I used to play darts with the sailors," he recalled. "As a young boy of 12 or 13, I got to be proficient."

This downtown gas station and shop was owned by the Whalens. All trace of it is gone. *Photo courtesy of Pete "Leo" Whalen*

The Whalens had another establishment next door, a gas station and convenience store (before the term "convenience store" had been coined). There, Whalen's father sold cigars, candy, soda, and gasoline – two or three brands. "Sky sailors," including German officers, would visit the shop to purchase American candy and other goods.

Despite having left town when he was about 14, Whalen can still recall the names and faces of children he used to play with as a boy, many from families whose names are etched upon tombstones at the old St. John's Church on Center Street, where Whalen attended mass. The church in which Whalen attended mass, and around which so many of the families he once knew are buried, is not home to the Lakehurst Historical Society.

In 1932, a new church arrived on the scene to build a whole new set of memories. That year, the Cathedral of the Air was constructed on Lakehurst-Whitesville Road, aka Route 547, just a few yards outside of town. Civic organizations such as the American Legion helped raise funds for its construction. The cathedral is well known for its gorgeous gothic architecture and has long been a popular place to get married.

Near the church, which is tucked between the edges of the borough and the Navy base, is another area about which longtime residents have fond memories. Stretching along the land behind the Lakehurst Diner, Burger King and other establishments on Route 70 were a series of cranberry bogs. They stretched out in a neat row, one next to the other. Those bogs are now overgrown swampland, but if you're willing to brave some wet shoes you can still see the rough borders of several bogs behind the homes along Manapaqua Avenue.

Larrabee C. Lillie, grandson of Edward Larrabee Sr., remembers his days playing in those bogs and the woods surrounding them. They were owned by residents – Harry Brant, Charlie Roberts, and others – and linked up to form a chain of bogs along the north side of the borough. In the 20s, 30s, and 40s, many of Lakehurst's youth would ice skate on the bogs during the winter, including one owned by Lillie's grandfather.

TRIVIA TIDBIT: Lillie reports that during his youth, "We used to call it Shanty Town by the train tracks."

Whalen recalled the same. "We would ice skate there, especially the one right where the Gulf station is. On the other corner at McDonald's, there was a little diner there."

Boating was also a popular recreation. For Lillie, Whalen, and others, those bogs were a big part of being young in Lakehurst. They provided a place for fishing, boating, skating, and even off-road driving.

"My grandfather came here in 1870 from Maine. He had it (the bog) before I was born. He had a bog over in Whitings, too," Lillie said. "That was a playground for me. I remember having an old Model T stripped down. We used to ford the stream and run it around on the sandy roads."

For the Pine Barrens, cranberry bogs are nothing unusual. They continue to dot the landscape, including in the Lakehurst area. To this day, nestled just over the Manchester border and under the shadow of the Navy base, a series of bogs are in constant operation, supplying the modern world's most recognizable cranberry-product producer, Ocean Spray, with bitter fruit. Located off Proving Grounds Road, those bogs have operated since at least the early 1950s, when they were owned by the Switlik family of Jackson. The

Lipman family purchased the property, now run by Jeff and Ned Lipman, more than a half century ago.

Cranberry cultivation in New Jersey dates back to the 1600s, when wild cranberries were a fruit of choice for both natives and settlers. By the mid-1800s, farmers began to raise cranberries in earnest, beginning, according to some local historians, in Pemberton. "People began to transplant then to the cleared and excavated bogs where ore raisers has removed bog iron," McPhee wrote, "and that was the beginning of commercial cranberry growing in the Pine Barrens." In 1869, the American Cranberry Growers was formed, an organization that still exists to this day. Before long, half of all cranberries grown in America were grown in New Jersey. Lakehurst was part of that thriving market.

"Working the cranberry bogs provided yearly fall jobs for most of the original Pineys," according to William McMahon. "The first berries were harvested by workers wading knee-deep in the bogs, armed with wooden scoops.

While no longer dominating the national market as before, cranberry growing remains a big industry in New Jersey – even if it's hard to tell from the rows of strip malls in Ocean County.

"New Jersey is third in the nation," Bill Lindley told this author. When I spoke to Lindley in 2005, his job was to keep an eye on the equipment and property at the Lipman fields located just outside of town. Currently, New Jersey has about 3,600 acres devoted to cranberry farming, compared to 11,000 in Massachusetts. That's down from well over 9,000 acres in New Jersey about 100 years ago.

But for young people in Lakehurst, the finer details of cranberry growing were not important. What was important was the fun and freedom those open stretches of land provided – and in some areas still provide today.

Yet in the early days of the 20th Century, "freedom" was a relative term. Even with wide bogs and untamed forest to enjoy, Lakehurst remained a small town with small town needs and small town services. For instance, if the town's youth got hurt while driving their Model Ts in ways Henry Ford never intended, they would have small town help. In the years leading up to World War II, most Lakehurst residents were familiar with the name Harold E. Pittis. He was a doctor in town until his death in 1938, doing his part to keep residents' health in check. A county historical sites survey indicates Pittis was "the only physician within a 24-mile area encompassing Lakehurst, Whiting and Chatsworth (Burlington County). He had an agreement with the railroad to be in this area, and would pay housecalls via bicycle and railroad handcar."

Pittis, whose house can still be seen at 297 Union Avenue, contributed to his community in other ways. He served as mayor from 1932 to 1935, etching his name into Lakehurst history in a very real way.

But the days of housecalls via bicycle would become more and more a quaint throwback to years gone by. The days of the Great Depression were being left behind. War loomed in Europe. Once again, the world was changing.

And as always, Lakehurst would not remain untouched by these changes.

A Profile in Hospitality

I don't remember exactly when I interviewed Leo Whalen. Circa 2004, I believe, when I was in the midst of the first expansion of what had started as a series of four or five articles for *The Manchester Times*, a weekly newspaper operating on Union Avenue in Lakehurst.

No, I don't remember when I interviewed him (and am too lazy to check those old, old notes), but I remember the interview like it was yesterday.

As the stories in this book make clear, Whalen had vivid memories of his time in Lakehurst. By the time I had caught up with him, however, he was happily retired and splitting time between a lovely home in Seaside Park and a winter home elsewhere. Seaside Park was a natural fit for him because it put him close to the Seaside Heights boardwalk, where the business he founded, Lucky Leo's, was being run by his son. The plan was to meet Leo at his shore home.

But there was a problem. My son, Robert, was young at the time and since mom was also busy that day, the poor kid was stuck tagging along with his dear old dad. "Mr. Whalen, I'll be there in an hour, but, ummm … would it be a terrible burden if I brought my son?"

Quite unprofessional of me. You just don't do these things. Leo did not bat an eye. In fact, he was thrilled at the idea.

Robert and I arrived and we were greeted by Leo and his wife as if we were old friends. Sit down. What would you like to drink? Would you like a sandwich? Come look at our pictures! They were like an aunt and uncle I hadn't realized I had.

I'm not sure how long we talked. It was a while. The Whalens loved to tell stories. We drifted off topic many times. Many, many times. I didn't mind. They were kind people by any measure. Robert, as well behaved even as a young child as he is now – credit mom for managing that trick, because dad was a hellraiser – enjoyed looking at the old pictures and hearing the stories and watching dad work. Even when the interview had run its course, the Whalens were ready to socialize.

When the time came to depart, something struck Leo. "Your son likes games, doesn't he?"

"What do you mean?"

"The boardwalk. He's played games down there?"

"Sure, we've gone as a family. He loves them."

So Leo insisted on calling his son, who was hard at working managing Lucky Leo's, and telling him that some friends were coming by. Treat them right, he instructed. I said I couldn't accept. He insisted. Robert seemed excited, so why not?

We ended up at Lucky Leo's on the famous Seaside Heights boardwalk, playing skeeball and arcade games and having a wonderful father and son afternoon … all on Leo. It's still a fond memory.

I don't know where Leo Whalen is today. It's been a number of years of work and family and writing and more. I just lost track of him. Maybe he's still in Seaside Park enjoying a quiet life. I hope so. Because if Leo Whalen is an example of what Lakehurst has produced, Lakehurst has every reason to be proud.

Yet this experience wasn't unusual. As I did interviews for a first series of 2002 articles on the history of Lakehurst, and then again for the second round of stories a few years later, and then yet <u>again</u> as I expanded that series of stories into this manuscript, time and again I was met with graciousness and hospitality. Marshall Sewell, Verna Thomas, Gladys Prosperi, Aurora Semple, John Iannaccone, Larrabee C. Lillie and far too many others to remember. All good people who gave of their time with great generosity.

Lakehurst may have produced some great stories, as I hope this book showcases, but it has also produced some great <u>people</u>.

THE WAR YEARS AND BEYOND

It was an early morning in the late 1930s. Erv Clement, division fire warden, leaves his home in Crestwood and makes for the Lakehurst Naval Air Station. There, he climbs the stairs to the top of Hangar No. 1. It is the peak of the fire season and this was the best way to survey the area. A train had just passed through the area, spewing smoke and belching fire. Now is a time of great risk.

Sure enough, there is smoke in the woods.

"We've got a burn going just south of Whitings," Clement would tell Marshall Sewell, then a reporter for the *Lakewood Daily Times*. "The 10:48 out of Lakehurst just went through."

It was not an uncommon occurrence. When the trains would pass through the pines, especially during April and May, "the steam locomotives would shower sparks on the right-of-way, even though their smokestacks had screens that were supposed to have prevented this," Sewell recalled.

So for the area's local reporter, it was off to cover the fire.

Such fires may have gotten people talking, but they were rarely a calamity. In the Pine Barrens, fires are only a temporary setback. In fact, the scrub pines unique to the area *require* the seasonal blazes in order to reproduce; their pine cones only open under intense heat, and the fire helps clear out competing trees. Visit an area through which fire has swept, and just a week or two later, green everywhere. In the pines fires do not destroy, they cleanse.

Some might argue that during this time, the 20th Century was a forest fire sweeping through Lakehurst.

In 1943, the last student attended classes at the old Lakehurst schoolhouse. No more single-room school for the young people of town. The move was part of a national trend. Such schools were disappearing across the country. For a new generation,

The old Lakehurst public school

Photo courtesy of Lakehurst Historical Society

tales of learning in a one-room school would be just another kooky story told my grandma and grandpa.

In 1945, Leo Whalen's father sold the establishment he built. It would later become Weaver's – still a hometown tavern filled with people who knew one another's name, but one step removed from its origins. And soon, the Whalen's left the borough behind, too. So did others. Many of their names are etched upon the gravestones at the old Roman Catholic church on Center Street. Families outgrew Lakehurst, or looked elsewhere for greener pastures. The little village that could was growing stagnant. Opportunities were few and modest. There was no rope factory. No Pine Tree Inn. Cargo trains still rolled through town, of course, and Navy Lakehurst continued operating, but good jobs? Not in this town.

Through the 1940s and into the 1950s, Lakehurst was a 19th Century town entering the 20th Century, a situation far from unique in the Pine Barrens, removed from the urban landscape as it was. A new phenomenon would begin inching across the landscape of 1950s America – the suburbs. Once all but isolated save for the tracks that snaked through the forest, Lakehurst was connecting with the surrounding region, and the surrounding region to Lakehurst.

Connections came in ways great and small. Students from town went to high school in Lakewood. High school photos from the era are littered with names from the borough. The 1936 state champion varsity football team out of Lakewood, for instance, included Earl Childers. The Childers family has been a Lakehurst mainstay for generations. For a time, the area was home to a baseball league made up of teams from Whiting, Mt. Holly, New Egypt, Toms River, Pleasant Plains, Lakewood and more. A squad from Lakehurst offered up some competition, becoming the Ocean County champions in 1940 and 1956, and the Tri-County champs in 1957. More and more, Lakehurst's small town flavor was being intermingled with the surrounding region.

Meanwhile, as World War II escalated and the attack at Pearl Harbor pulled America into war, Lakehurst found its military role growing increasingly important. The base was already the center of airship operations on the East Coast. War forced it to grow to accommodate that role. The borough was quickly becoming a key component in America's efforts during World War II.

In 1942, Hangars 2 and 3 were built next to Hangar No. 1, immediately followed the next year by Hangars 5 and 6. Those two massive wooden structures came during a flurry of wartime construction. Seventeen in all were built; all but seven have since been knocked down. As the war peaked, so did the base. Lighter-than-air flights to the North Atlantic and Europe were commissioned out of Lakehurst. At any given time, upwards of 27 blimps could be operating out of Lakehurst at once. The base's home squadron, Airship Squadron Twelve (ZP-12), flew over 5,000 submarine patrol sorties before the war ended in 1945. Blimps were now capable of landing on aircraft carrier decks. During the war, Goodyear Corp. built well over 100 airships for use during World War II. Gone were the enormous rigid airships of the 1930s. These were smaller and lighter, little different than the Goodyear blimps still seen today. The K-type ships were capable of staying aloft for 40 hours, making them a perfect patrol blimp. They helped in anti-submarine combat, escorted convoys of ships, conducted rescue missions at sea, and did general patrol/recon work.

Accidents still happened. On June 8, 1942, two blimps out of Lakehurst collided over the Manasquan Inlet. Ten were killed. But as always, the Navy soldiered on. According to Naval historians

Pace, Montgomery and Zitarosa, "During the war, blimps safely escorted 89,000 surface ships in all kinds of weather, around the clock, often when airplanes were grounded. Only one blimp is confirmed lost to enemy action, but one-fifth of the Navy's blimps were damaged, ripped or wrecked beyond repair in operational mishaps."

In ways great and small, Navy Lakehurst was still making an impact. But its role, like the role of the town it called home, was changing, too.

While airships flew over the frigid waters of the Atlantic, spying out German submarines, some of the first steps were being taken on the grounds of Navy Lakehurst to develop a new kind of aircraft. Something new. And decidedly modern.

The helicopter. In 1947, the Navy's first ever helicopter squadrons were formed — and they were formed right in Lakehurst. Soon, chopper training missions would be on the rise while airship missions would be on the decline. The entire role of Navy Lakehurst was at the start of a transformation that would take over a decade. A parachute rigger school was established there as early as 1924, but operations at the school surged as airship operations declined. By the 1950s, Navy and Marine parachuters were packing their own chutes and making high altitude jumps over Lakehurst.

Like the borough itself, even the Navy base was leaving yesterday behind. Lakehurst's days as a window into the late 19th Century were ending. They would soon be over.

INTO THE
MODERN ERA

In 1962, the last official U.S. Navy blimp flew from Lakehurst.

It had been a long time coming, but by this point it was inevitable. In 1961, the Navy had only 10 blimps in operation. The prior year, another blimp accident claimed 18 lives. More cuts followed. By August of the following year, the Navy had only two blimps, both stored at Hangar No. 1. In late 1962, the last Naval blimps were deflated.

That was it. The end. An era, over. The airships would no longer cruise majestically over Lakehurst. At least, not in an official military capacity. Those days were finished.

But that was not all bad, not for the people who made a living on the base. Even after airships lost their importance to the military, work at the base continued. The base at Lakehurst was founded as a center for airships and that's what it remained for decades, but the world of the military is adapt or die (both figuratively and literally). In the 60s, 70s, and 80s, as the role of airships in America's military faded and ultimately died, the base's mission evolved beyond lighter-than-air craft. Helicopter development and deployment, and later aircraft carrier technology, would jump to the forefront at Navy Lakehurst. Between the 1940s and the 1960s, important steps in the development of the helicopter took place in Lakehurst, and by the 1980s, key aircraft carrier technology was beginning to be developed there.

TRIVIA TIDBIT: Where today Lakehurst Hardware stands on Union Avenue used to be a Ford dealership. In fact, it was the original Downs Ford, a well-known dealership in Ocean County.

"Butch" White, who lived in town as a child, recalls swimming at Lake Horicon and watching Navy helicopters conduct

Eisenhower's was a famous - and sometimes infamous - establishment located on the outskirts of town. After fire gutted it, it was torn down. Today the La Bove Grande (once called the Circle Landmark) stands in its place. *Photo courtesy of Lakehurst Historical Society*

drills at the lake. Personnel would be dropped at the lake and await a helicopter to "rescue" them. Once, White claimed, he saw a chopper go down when its rotors hit the water. Both the crew and the men it was tasked with "rescuing" then needed rescue.

As the Cold War escalated, so did other testing and operations. Carrier Air Reserve Wing 70 operated largely out of Lakehurst, conducting anti-submarine patrols over the Atlantic. The Navy's only parachute rigger school operated in Lakehurst, too. It wasn't the base it had been.

But hi-tech developments on the nearby Naval base did not necessarily mean the same for Lakehurst. At heart it remained, and remains, a small Pine Barrens town.

In 1962, residents in town would call Harold J. Fuccile their mayor, his second time serving. His first tenure was from 1936 to 1939. Fuccile remains a familiar local name to this day; so, too, do the names of other past mayors: Charles L. Rogers from 1921 to 1924 (Lakehurst's first mayor), Harold Pittis from 1932 to 1935, Stephen Morris from 1942 to 1957, Charles Becker in 1958 and 1959, and others. The name Rogers still graces Union Avenue. The Morris family still lives in town. The Beckers lent their name to a section of Manchester, Beckerville.

Modern life did not mean small town life disappeared. Locals still gathered in area taverns for a few beers, waiting for hunting season or discussing their civil service job on the base, which had become (and remains) the area's largest employer.

For a time, life in Lakehurst meant doing your grocery shopping at IGA (Independent Grocers of America). The first IGA came in 1957 next to Borough Hall on Union Avenue. Joe and Ruth Sacco owned the store.

During this stretch of years, "Eisenhower's Musical Bar" was operating off what is now known as the Eisenhower Circle, the traffic circle nearest Whiting. It was a popular place for music, dance and camaraderie, and many longtime residents recall enjoying fun evenings there. The establishment would in its final years become more of a "biker bar," an ugly, seedy dive on the best of nights. It would eventually burn down in the mid 1980s. By the 1990s, the much classier Circle Landmark, now called the La Bove Grande, would replace it.

The cost to live in Lakehurst at the time? In the 1960s, homes along Willow and Poplar streets were selling for a robust $6,000.

Around this same time, just a few miles down highway 40 — it's now known as Route 70 — in a place then called Whitings, the Crestwood Village Development Company began buying up large tracts of land. That land would soon become the sprawling senior communities of nearby Whiting.

The Garden State Parkway now sliced its way through Ocean County, deeply transforming the landscape. The floodgates of tourism and commuting were open. New residents swarmed into the region. Good paying jobs in North Jersey beckoned. Isolation was no longer possible -- or desirable.

For Lakehurst, tomorrow was coming.

Over the course of the next several decades, the same would hold true for the county as a whole.

Through the 1960s, modern day America marched forward, with the Vietnam War, civil rights and The Beatles defining the era. For Lakehurst, though, the major steps forward were not as monumental. In 1967, the first sewer bonds were sold in town, paving the way (no pun intended) for city water and sewer. While well-water is still used in town, city water and sewer is now accessible to all borough residents. As big as The Beatles? Maybe not, but this helped prompt the borough's sharp housing expansion. These days, the Westlake portion of town — the duplex

By the middle of the 20th Century, ruins like these in between the spurs at Union Avenue were the few remaining reminders that Lakehurst was once a bustling railroad town

homes off Route 70, on the northeast side of town — is a familiar site. But in the 1960s, scrub pines still covered the area.

"When I first moved here in 1961, that was all woods," recalled Aurora Semple, a member of the Lakehurst Historical Society and once a familiar face at Lakehurst Elementary School.

But soon dozens of duplex houses were built, and families from North Jersey began to move into town. This author was among them. It was a new demographic for what had been a close-knit Pine Barrens community. The town was growing. And changing.

The IGA on Union Avenue moved to a plaza off Route 70, where it operated until the early 1990s, only to be closed and replaced by a Rite Aid pharmacy. It, too, closed its doors. That entire plaza is paved and packed with stores (or at times empty commercial space), but as recently as the 1980s, the entire parcel with the exception of the IGA was pine forest. The woods were adjacent to Westlake and for a time became a favorite beer drinking spot for underage youths. Pits filled with broken bottles and campfires littered the small clump of woods.

In the early 1970s, Luigi Bove came to town, bought an existing establishment, and planted the seeds for what would become Luigi's, now a staple of Lakehurst's Union Avenue downtown. Before and after, other businesses came, populating town with familiar storefronts still in business today. A car dealership departed Union Avenue and was replaced by Lakehurst Hardware (which has undergone several name changes over the years); the Placeks, a longtime Lakehurst family, founded Lakehurst Lawnmower; Hall's Gulf began pumping gas and towing cars; and too many others to mention, all names familiar to those who have been in town for years.

By this time, these were all familiar to the *author*. These were the building blocks of my Lakehurst.

In the 1980s, the buzzsaw sound of dirt bikes and ATVs became commonplace; tons of old stoves, refrigerators, and other trash were cleaned up from the lengthy unpaved stretch of Union Avenue leading to the back of the Navy base (called "Dais Road" by some, and marked on a 1908 map as "To New Egypt")); local firefighters still brought cases of beer to the scene of forest fires, older members gathering around at the scene and drinking Budweiser while the younger members put out the fire (a practice long since ceased); Eisenhower's was consumed by flame; stretches of woods were cleared near Eisenhower Circle for commercial construction, even as a gas station there went out of business; and

This Union Avenue tavern burned down in the 1980s. Today, a municipal parking lot stands in its place.
Photo courtesy of U.S. Register of Historic Places

the last air show in many years was held at Navy Lakehurst, the accidental death of a parachuter a grim highlight. It was a place of pickup trucks and tiny taverns. At any given time, there were half-a-dozen places to drink in the square-mile town. Those taverns were always balanced out by a similar number of churches, where the hungover could confess their sins.

There was even another airship disaster in Lakehurst, though few people saw this one. The Piasecki PA-97, better known as the Helistat, was an experimental airship being tested at Navy Lakehurst. It looked like any other airship, except it had four helicopters mounted below it off the four corners of the gondola. The idea was to give the airship greater lift. Plans called for the Forest Service to use it for its heavy lift capabilities.

"Designed in particular to haul great loads of timber out of inaccessible virgin forests," *The New York Times* wrote on July 2, 1986, "it combined a 343-foot-long, one-million-cubic-foot Dacron bag – about five times the volume of a Goodyear blimp – and four old navy helicopters."

Test flights with the Helistat began in late April, 1986. This author witnessed at least one flight, albeit from a distance, when he and a friend (Arthur Johnson, now of Georgia) snuck through the Lipman's cranberry bogs and to the back gate of the base to watch.

The Helistat would not last long. On July 1, 1986, a gust of strong wind began to shake the undercarriage holding the four helicopters. The structure of the craft wasn't prepared for the winds. In an instant they broke free, destroying the airship and killing one pilot, Gary Oleshfski, of Bordentown.

For many years the accident seemed like a big secret. Today, video of the crash can be viewed on Youtube.

And still Lakehurst carried on. Time marched forward. Americans were afraid of nuclear war. The Berlin Wall fell. "Born In The USA" topped the charts (but few people understood that it *wasn't* a patriotic song). People struggled to solve the Rubik's Cube. Ronald Reagan left office and George Bush became our president.

Without realizing quite how or when it happened, the people of Lakehurst found that tomorrow had become today.

LAKEHURST TODAY

It is the 21st Century.

Like so many things in this world, Lakehurst has changed. And yet so much has remained the same.

In many ways, the Lakehurst of the 21st Century is not much different than the Lakehurst of the 20th Century, or even the 19th Century. Entering the new millennium, the small Borough of Lakehurst remains exactly that. Small. The town is still fiercely independent. Talks about being reabsorbed into Manchester have remained little more than idle talk. And the "one big family" atmosphere has waned, yes, but hasn't disappeared altogether. People in town still know one another's name.

But that is not to say that nothing has changed.

Following the growth of the 60s and 70s, the demographic in town slowly shifted. Longtime families were replaced by new residents from elsewhere, largely North Jersey. By 2000, the borough had become a "bedroom community" where those who

Union Avenue in Lakehurst circa 2004

lived here worked elsewhere. People who both live and work in town are increasingly rare. Commuters are plentiful. Old families, families that have lived here as long as the pines ... they're still around, but not like before. Once the rule, they're now an exception.

For a time in the 70s and 80s, the borough was home to some semi-notorious taverns and nightspots. These days, those "trouble spots" have long since been closed down. In recent years, Route 70 development and downtown renovations have once again made Lakehurst a successful place to run a business.

The Navy base was always an important part of life in Lakehurst, quietly contributing to the U.S. Navy's mission on a daily basis. "For 30 years," noted historians Pace, Montogomery and Zitarosa, "every carrier deckhand in the U.S. Navy trained at Lakehurst." It continues to be important both locally and throughout the military today. In 1977, the base changed names. No longer was it the Naval Air Station, Lakehurst. Now, in order to reflect its new role in the military, it was the Naval Air Engineering Center, Lakehurst. Elected officials fought and won to increase the base's role in the military, giving new life and a new mission to the historic naval base. As rounds of closings threatened bases all across the nation, Lakehurst's role in the American Armed Forces was strengthened. The base's mission was given a boost when, in the first decade of the new millennium, it joined with Fort Dix and McGuire Air Force base to become "Joint Base McGuire-Dix-Lakehurst," the nation's first "super base." Today, the base is a vital part of developing launch and safety technology for aircraft carriers.

And as of this writing, trains may be returning to Lakehurst. Not right away, not even tomorrow, but ten, maybe fifteen years from now ... maybe.

Not likely. But maybe.

Many say that Lakehurst is a community on the upswing, looking toward a brighter tomorrow. All signs seem to indicate some truth to that. The return of rail service will be an integral part of the process, but even now members of the local business community are ensuring blood continues to pump in the town's old veins.

It hasn't been easy. Lakehurst is contained by tight boundaries. There is little expansion left for this tiny town. A new strip mall on Route 70 opened its doors at the end of the first decade of the century, the first major growth the town had seen in years. It's a bit ugly, looking not unlike every other strip mall in a state blanketed with them, but there are local business owners there who seem eager to become part of the community. Maybe they'll contribute to the character of the town in a positive way. Only time will tell.

Union Avenue looks different in the new century, too. Sprawling Victorian homes that had fallen into disrepair were scooped up by eager buyers (one of them former mayor Stephen Childers) and renovated. Drive past Lakehurst Elementary School these days and every home you see is worth envying. It's a marked

These days, the railroad tracks running through Lakehurst are almost always devoid of activity. A movement to return passenger trains to the area began in the 2000s but as of this writing appeared to be a lost cause.

difference from years past.

And in recent years, the hushed talk has been about Hibernia Avenue, a one-block stretch of road few outside of town ever see. Linking Route 70 and Center Street, the homes here were built in the 19th Century by Irish immigrants working William Torrey's railroad. The rumor is that town officials want those homes gone. In their place? Another strip mall, they secretly hope.

This is what they call progress.

Even through change; through evolution; through the shifts time brings, the people of Lakehurst continue to treasure their town's special place in history. Lakehurst is filled with more stories than this book can tell. Many of those stories are told in the Lakehurst Historical Society Museum, located on Center Street just across from the firehouse. Opened in 1993, the museum is a window to Lakehurst's past, and a place to preserve the artifacts that make the community what it is today. Items displaying the borough's history going back to the Civil War are there for the curious to see and handle. To *experience*. From old books and township records, tools from yesteryear, and scores of photographs showing the Lakehurst railroad's heyday, as well as clothing and toys from the earlier part of the century, there is plenty on-hand to absorb. Visitors to the museum will find an old jail cell, a slew of items from the Pine Tree Inn, baseball uniforms, memorabilia from the fire department, old borough records, and much more. Like Lakehurst itself, it's a small place yet is packed with history.

And most important of all, the museum has *people*, people who can share stories of days long since past, but not quite forgotten.

What will Lakehurst be tomorrow? No one can tell. Borough residents will certainly be lucky if the next 100 years have as many interesting tales to tell as the last 100, or the 100 before that. The only thing for certain is that there will be change. Always change. The face of the community will be familiar ... yet different.

So Lakehurst has always been. And so Lakehurst shall always be.

This bare patch of land behind the Union Avenue municipal parking lot was once home to a train station. That past is gone. But it is not forgotten.

SOURCES &
BIBLIOGRAPHY

In addition to countless interviews and general research, a number of other sources provided the backbone for this book. They are covered here as completely as possible. Apologies in advance for inevitable oversights. When it comes to photos, credit is given based on where the author obtained the photo, and photos themselves, even those in the public domain, are credited whenever possible. For credit on photos erroneously listed in the public domain or otherwise incorrectly credited, contact the author at ericsanjuan@gmail.com.

THE FEDERAL FORGE
AND EARLY LAKEHURST

McPhee, John, *The Pine Barrens*, (Farrar, Straus and Giroux 1978)

Boyer, Charles S., *Early Forges and Furnaces in New Jersey* (original 1931, University of Pennsylvania Press reprint, 1963)

Dewey, William S., *Early Manchester and William Torrey, (Manchester Publishing Co., 1981)*

Solem-Stull, Barbara, *Ghost Towns and Other Quirky Places in the New Jersey Pine Barrens*, (Plexus Publishing Inc., 2005)

Wilson, Harold F., *The Jersey Shore: a Social and Economic History of the Counties of Atlantic, Cape May, Monmouth and Ocean*, (Lewis Historical Publishing, 1953)

Vei, Richard F., *New Jersey Cemeteries and Tombstones: History in the Landscape* (Rutgers University Press, 2008)

McMahon, William, *Pine Barrens Legends & Lore*, (Middle Atlantic Press, 1987)

Torrey, Frederic Crosby, *Souvenir of Lakehurst: History of the pine region of New Jersey*, (self-published, 1908)

Beck, Henry Charlton, *Forgotten Towns of Southern New Jersey*, (Rutgers University press, 1983)

WILLIAM TORREY, KING OF THE PINES

Dewey, *Early Manchester*

New York Tribune, September 10, 1862

Treese, Lorett, *Railroads of New Jersey: Fragments of the Past in the Garden State Landscape* (Stackpole Books 2006)

END OF AN EMPIRE

Wainwright, Frank, *Advance Nickel News*, 1971

Barber, John N. and Howe, Henry, *Historical Collections of the State of New Jersey*, (1868)

Dewey, *Early Manchester*

LARABEES, LONGCHAMPS & LABORERS

Torrey, *Souvenir of Lakehurst*

THE RUSSIANS COME TO TOWN

Montgomery, Ronald; Pace, Kevin; and Zitarosa, Rick, piece for Navy Lakehurst Historical Society

ENTER THE AIRSHIPS

Montgomery, Ronald; Pace, Kevin; and Zitarosa, Rick, *Naval Air Station, Lakehurst*, (Arcadia Publishing, 2003)

TOWERS IN THE PINES

National Register of Historic Places nomination, 2001

Pine Tree Inn brochure

Torrey, *Souvenir of Lakehurst*

LIGHTER THAN AIR

McPhee, *Pine Barrens*

LAST DAYS OF THE PINE TREE INN

Barbaccia, Annette, report for NJ Pinelands Commission, 2001

THE TITANIC OF THE SKIES

Morrison, Herbert & Nehlson, Charlie, radio broadcast for WLS Chicago

LAST DAYS OF THE RAILROAD

Treese, *Railroads of New Jersey*

Caldes, Charles P., *Steam to Diesel in New Jersey* (Arcadia Publishing 2002)

Bianculli, Anthony J., *Iron Rails in the Garden State: Tales of New Jersey Railroading* (Indiana University Press 2008)

INTO THE MODERN ERA

Special to the New York Times, *The New York Times*, July 2, 1986

LAKEHURST TODAY

Montgomery, Ronald; Pace, Kevin; and Zitarosa, Rick, Navy Lakehurst Historical Society

ABOUT THE AUTHOR

 **E**ric San Juan spent his formative years romping around the woods of Lakehurst, troubling the teachers of its elementary school, and dreaming of getting out of the town he'd eventually come to love. Yet come to love it he would. After graduating from Lakehurst Elementary School in 1987 and Manchester Township High School in 1991, Eric returned to Lakehurst in 1999 when he took a position at the local newspaper, *The Manchester Times*. This book began there.

He is the author of *Stuff Every Husband Should Know* (Quirk Books 2011), coauthor of *A Year of Hitchcock: 52 Weeks with the Master of Suspense* (Scarecrow Press 2009) and contributing author on *Geek Wisdom: The Sacred Teachings of Nerd Culture* (Quirk Book 2011). He is the author and creator of the *Pitched!* series of comic anthologies, which include a story inspired by his time in Lakehurst ("The End of All Summers," illustrated by James Pipik). His work has appeared in *Weird Tales, Boston Literary Magazine*, and other publications. He can be heard with Jim McDevitt on the official Year of Hitchcock podcast (ayearofhitchcock.com).

Eric dearly misses hiking in the woods surrounding Lakehurst.

He can be reached at ericsanjuan@gmail.com. More information can be found at www.ericsanjuan.com.

Other Works by Eric San Juan

Stuff Every Husband Should Know
(Quirk Books 2011)

Pitched! Volume 1: Nine Stories
(self-published)

Pitched! Volume 2: Seven More Stories
(self-published)

With Jim McDevitt

A Year of Hitchcock:
52 Weeks with the Master of Suspense
(Scarecrow Press 2009)

With Stephen Segal (editor and coauthor)
and Zaki Hasan; N.K.; Jemisin; and Genevieve Valentine
(coauthors).

Geek Wisdom: The Sacred Teachings of Nerd Culture
(Quirk Books 2011)